Preface

Sport is a contest of person against person or team against team. A Sport consists of freedoms, barriers and purposes, and there is a necessity in a game to have an opponent or an enemy. Also there is a necessity to have problems, and enough individuality to cope with a situation.

There are many sports played throughout the world. Different sports require different types of arenas, different types of sports equipments, and different number of players. A single sport can be played in different countries but the motto of every sport is to generate sportsman spirit among the players.

Every sport requires a mental and physical fitness. Some games are played by mental fitness like chess while some requires only physical strength as in weightlifting and others are combination of both like soccer, hockey etc. Different games are played for different duration of time like boxing round is for few minutes while a lawn tennis set can vary from few minutes to hours.

For smooth flow of game an official is required. This official closely observes that a game is played within the globally accepted rules. This official is called Umpire or Referee. The international body of that particular sport appoints these officials. Such officials are well versed with the rules of the game.

A grand event is held after every four years known as Olympics. In this events all the games, which are played throughout the world, are included. Participants from all over the globe, work hard to qualify for the Olympics. Every Olympic participant has to qualify through pre-Olympic qualifiers.

This book is a collection of all the terms used in different sports like badminton, cricket, basketball, fencing, rowing, ice hockey, field hockey, weight lifting etc. It also explains about the various equipments used in different games.

Lotus Illustrated DICTIONARY of SPORTS

Complied and Edited by:
Jamie Striesend

Lotus PRESS
4735/22, Prakash Deep Building
Ansari Road, Daryaganj,
New Delhi - 110002

Lotus Illustrated

DICTIONARY of SPORTS

ISBN 81 89093 61 4

Published by:

Lotus Press Publishers & Distributors
Unit No. 220, 2nd Floor, 4735/22,
Prakash Deep Building, Ansari Road, Darya Ganj,
New Delhi- 110002, Ph.: 32903912, 23280047, 09811838000
• E-mail : lotuspress1984@gmail.com www.lotuspress.co.in

Printed at : Lotus Press Publishers & Distributors, New Delhi

■ 1-and-1 or 1-plus-1 (basketball)
a free-throw attempt awarded for certain violations that earns the shooter a 2nd attempt only if the first is successful.

■ 2-point conversion (football)
when a team that just scored a touchdown starts a play at the opponent's 2-yard line and crosses the goal line to earn 2 points; when successful, it looks just like a touchdown; introduced to the NFL in 1994.

■ 3-on-3 (basketball)
a game played with only 3 players on the court for each team.

■ 3-point play (basketball)
a 2-point field goal followed by a successful free-throw.

■ 3-point shot (basketball)
a field goal worth 3 points because the shooter had both feet on the floor behind the 3-point line when he released the ball; also counts if one foot is behind the line while the other is in the air.

■ 4-point play (basketball)
a 3-point shot followed by a successful free-throw.

■ absence of blade (fencing)
when the blades are not touching; opposite of engagement.

■ accidentally offside (rugby)
a player is accidentally offside if he cannot avoid contact with an opponent while being offside. A scrummage is formed at the place where his team last played the ball.

■ ace (lawn tennis)
a serve that the opponent cannot return; as a verb, to serve an ace.

■ ace (table tennis)
a serve that cannot be reached by the opponent.

■ action (wrestling)
the referee's command to begin wrestling.

■ ad (lawn tennis)
short for advantage; see entries beginning with that word, below.

■ ad (table tennis)
short for advantage.

■ ad in (table tennis)
indicates that the server has the advantage.

■ ad out (table tennis)
indicates that the player returning serve has the advantage.

■ adams division (icehockey)
with the Patrick Division made up the Wales Conference until the 1992-93 season; renamed the Northeast Division of the Eastern Conference starting with the 1993-94 season.

■ advance (fencing)
a movement forward by step, cross or balestra.

■ advance (field hockey)
to push, shove or advance the ball in any way, using body, hands or feet rather than the stick. Advancing is a foul.

■ advantage (lawn tennis)
the player who scores the first point after deuce is said to have the advantage, since winning the next point will also win the game.

■ advantage (rugby)
a principle of officiating: the referee allows the game to proceed unless a major infraction occurs; a minor infraction will not stop play if the non-offending team gains an advantage. An advantage may be territorial or may consist in gaining possession of the ball.

■ advantage (table tennis)
the player who scores the first point after deuce is said to have the advantage.

■ advantage court (lawn tennis)
the left service court, where the receiver takes service when either player has the advantage.

■ advantage in (lawn tennis)
indicates that the server has the advantage; also *ad in.*

■ advantage out (lawn tennis)
indicates that the receiver has the advantage; also *ad out.*

■ advantage rule (water polo)
a rule that a referee should refrain from calling a foul if the call would be to the advantage of the offender's team.

■ aerial (gymnastics)
a skill performed without the hands touching the floor or the apparatus. Also used as an adjective, as in aerial cartwheel and aerial walkover.

■ aero bar (cycling)
a handlebar that juts forward so that the rider can assume a low profile for better aerodynamics.

■ aid (equestrian)
any signal given to a horse to prompt it to turn, change gaits or perform some other maneuver. *See natural aids.*

■ aids (fencing)
the last three fingers of the sword hand.

■ aikido (martial arts)
a martial art, based on older styles of ju-jitsu, created by Ueshiba Morihei in the 20th century. Japanese for the way of harmony.

■ aligner (rowing)
an official who's responsible for aligning boats evenly evenly for a fair start.

■ aligner's hut (rowing)
a hut or gazebo on the starting line, occupied by the starting judge and the aligner.

■ alive (basketball)
a ball is alive when it is released by a shooter or thrower or legally tapped by a jumper during a jump ball; the game clock starts only when the ball becomes alive; compare with live.

■ all (lawn tennis)
used in scoring to indicate a tie, as in 40-all.

■ alley (lawn tennis)
one of the areas outside the singles court that come into play in doubles. The alleys are 4 ½ feet wide.

■ **alleys (badminton)**
the areas, 1 $^{1}/_{2}$ feet wide on each side of the court that are used for doubles play.

■ **all-star game (icehockey)**
a mid-season exhibition game pitting selected stars of North American origin against selected stars from the rest of the World; from 1969 to 1997, the game was played between representatives from the NHL's two conferences.

■ **alternating-possession rule (basketball)**
the possession arrow changes direction after each subsequent jump ball situation, alternating which team gets possession for the throw-in.

■ **American twist (lawn tennis)**
a serve that has spin causing it to bounce high and to receiver's left, off a right-handed player's racket. Opposite of reverse twist.

■ **amplitude (gymnastics)**
height, speed or vigour in the execution of a movement. Generally, higher amplitude results in a higher score.

■ **analysis (fencing)**
reconstruction of the fencing phrase to determine priority of touches.

■ **ankle lace (wrestling)**
a hold in which the wrestler grasps the opponent by the ankles with his arms and exposes the opponent's back to the mat.

■ **anti-spin rubber (table tennis)**
a slick rubber that has little reaction to spin on the opponent's shot.

■ **apparatus (gymnastics)**
one of the pieces of equipment used in gymnastics competition, including the balance beam, the horizontal bar, parallel bars, the pommel horse, still rings, uneven bars and the vaulting horse.

■ **appeal (cricket)**
a claim that a batter has been put out, made by the person making the play. (Umpires will not signal some outs unless appealed to, by the appropriate player).

■ **approach shot (lawn tennis)**
a shot hit hard and deep to allow the player to take the net.

■ **arch (gymnastics)**
a position in which the body is curved backwards.

■ **arm bar (wrestling)**
a method of turning an opponent from stomach to back on the mat by wrapping an arm around the opponent's elbow and using the leverage of that hold to flip him over.

■ **arm throw (wrestling)**
a move in which a wrestler throws the opponent over his shoulder by holding the opponent's arm.

■ **around-the-head (badminton)**
a shot often used to avoid the backhand. It's similar to the overhead smash, but the shuttlecock is struck on the opposite side of the head from the player's racket hand.

■ **ashi waza (martial arts)**
leg techniques, including kicks and throws in which the pivot point is the leg or foot.

■ **assault (fencing)**
friendly combat between two fencers.

■ **assist (baseball)**
help from a fielder in putting an offensive player out. A fielder is credited with an assist when he throws a baserunner or hitter out at a base.

■ **assist (basketball)**
the last pass to a teammate that leads directly to a field goal; the scorer must move immediately toward the basket for the passer to be credited with an assist; only 1 assist can be credited per field goal.

■ **assist (icehockey)**
the pass or passes which immediately precede a successful scoring attempt; a maximum of two assists are credited for one goal.

■ **astroturf (football)**
an artificial surface used instead of grass on many football fields.

■ **at bat (baseball)**
the offensive team's turn to bat the ball and score. Each player takes a turn at bat until three outs are made. Each batter's opportunity at the plate is scored as an at bat for him.

■ **atemi waza (martial arts)**
striking techniques, including kicks, punchesand blocks.

■ **attack (cycling)**
a sudden burst of speed designed to leave a rider or group of riders behind. As a verb, to attempt an attack.

■ **attack (fencing)**
the initial offensive action made by extending the sword arm and continuously threatening the valid target of the opponent.

■ **attack au fer (fencing)**
an attack that is prepared by deflecting the opponent's blade, eg. beat, press, froissement.

■ **attack the net (lawn tennis)**
see *take the net.*

■ **attacker (field hockey)**
see *forward.*

■ **attacker (table tennis)**
a player, who tries to overpower opponents by killing as many balls as possible.

■ **attacking team (water polo)**
the team that has control of the ball. In the case of a free ball, the team that last had possession. Opposite of defensive team.

■ **attacking zone (icehockey)**
the area between the opponents' blue line and their goal.

■ attempt (weightlifting)
each lifter is allowed three attempts, at requested weights, on the snatch and on the clean and jerk. The results of the best good lifts are added to reach a total. If the lifter doesn't have at least one valid attempt in each of the two lifts, there is no total.

■ attempt board (weightlifting)
an electronically-controlled display that shows the name of the competitor, the weight division, the lift being attempted, the number of the attempt and the weight to be lifted. The referee decision lights and timing clock are also shown on the attempt board.

■ audible (football)
verbal commands shouted by the quarterback to his teammates at the line of scrimmage to change a play on short notice.

■ back (rugby)
one of the players usually numbered 9 through 15. Except for the scrumhalf, backs don't take part in scrums or lineouts.

■ back court (lawn tennis)
the area of the court from the baseline to the service line.

■ back giant (gymnastics)
a giant that begins with the body moving backward.

■ back handspring (gymnastics)
a back flip using both hands on the floor or apparatus, beginning and ending in a standing position. The legs come over the head as a unit.

■ back line (field hockey)
one of two lines marking the lengthwise boundaries of the field. The goal line is the section of the back line between the goal posts.

■ back row (rugby)
the two flankers and the No. 8 man, lined up for a scrum.

■ **back splash (rowing)**
spray toward the bow from an oar that enters the water on recovery.

■ **back walkover (gymnastics)**
a move that begins with a back arch or bridge position, in which one foot is brought down to the front, followed by the other foot.

■ **backboard (basketball)**
the rectangular structure, 6' x 3 1/2', to which the basket is attached.

■ **backboard (lawn tennis)**
a wall, usually of wood that's used for practice. It's often marked with a line at the height of the net.

■ **backcheck (icehockey)**
an attempt by a player, on his way back to his defensive zone, to regain the puck from the opposition by checking or harassing an opponent who has the puck.

■ **backcourt (badminton)**
the back third of the court.

■ **backcourt (basketball)**
the area from the midcourt line to the end line furthest from the offense's basket.

■ **backfield (football)**
the area behind the line of scrimmage.

■ **backhand (lawn tennis)**
a shot hit from the wrong side of the body, i.e., the side away from the racket; the left side for a right-handed player.

■ **backhand (table tennis)**
a shot hit on the opposite side of the body from the

racket hand; the left side, for a right-handed player.

■ **backhand (water polo)**
a shot or pass that's flipped backward, over the shoulder or head.

■ **backhand shot (icehockey)**
a shot or pass made with the stick from the left side by a right-handed player or from the right side by a left-handed player.

■ **back-in, full-out (gymnastics)**
a double salto with a full twist, the twist completed during the second salto. Compare full-in, back-out.

■ **backs (football)**
the running backs; the halfback and the fullback.

■ **backspin (lawn tennis)**
backward rotation on the ball, caused by drawing the racket strings down during the stroke that results in a low bounce. On some surfaces, the ball may even bounce back toward the net. Also known as underspin. See also *chip; chop.*

■ **backspin (table tennis)**
reverse spin applied by drawing the face of the racket down across the ball at impact. Also called underspin.

■ **backstop (lawn tennis)**
a fence, wall or other boundary behind the end of the court that retains balls within a limited area.

■ **backstop (rowing)**
a small block on the bow end of the slide, which holds the seat on track.

■ **backstop (baseball)**
fence or wall behind home plate.

■ **backsword (fencing)**
an archaic, edged, unpointed sword used in prize fighting; also singlestick.

■ **balance beam (gymnastics)**
1. A piece of apparatus 120 centimeters high, 10 centimeters wide and 500 centimeters long.

2. A women's event performed on the apparatus. The balance beam routine lasts 70 to 90 seconds and includes a variety of acrobatic, gymnastic and dance moves, ending with a dismount.

■ balestra (fencing)
a forward hop or jump, typically followed by an attack such as a lunge or fleche.

■ balk (baseball)
(Call of Umpire) Penalty for an illegal movement by the pitcher. The rule is designed to prevent pitchers from deliberately deceiving the runners.

■ balk (equestrian)
to stop short of an obstacle.

■ ball (baseball)
(Call of Umpire) A pitch outside the strike zone.

■ ball (field hockey)
field hockey uses a ball of solid plastic, with a circumference of 8 13/16 to 9 ¼ inches, weighing between 5 ½ and 5 ¾ ounces.

■ ball (table tennis)
the table tennis ball is a hollow sphere of celluloid or similar plastic, 40 millimeters in diameter and 2.7 grams in weight.

■ ball (water polo)
the ball used in water polo is a pressurised sphere weighing 400 to 450 grams. For men's play, it is .68 to .71 meters in circumference and inflated to 13-14 pounds of pressure. For women's play, it is .65 to .78 meters in circumference and inflated to 12-13 pounds of pressure.

■ ball boy/girl (lawn tennis)
a youngster who retrieves balls, usually from errant serves, to keep the court clear during a match.

■ ball carrier (football)
any player who has possession of the ball.

■ ball handler (basketball)
the player with the ball; usually the point guard at the start of a play.

■ ball toss (lawn tennis)
the action of tossing the ball into the air to initiate a serve.

■ ball under (water polo)
a foul committed when a player for takes or holds the ball underwater while being tackled by an opponent.

■ band (lawn tennis)
the strip of canvas at the top of the net.

■ bank shot (basketball)
a shot where the ball is first bounced (or banked) off the backboard at such an angle that it then drops into the basket.

■ bar (weightlifting)
short for *barbell.*

■ barbell (weightlifting)
the entire bar that is lifted, including the weight discs and collars.

■ base (baseball)
one of four stations to be reached in turn by the runner.

■ base coach (baseball)
a coach who stands by first or third base. The base coaches instruct the batter and base runners with a series of hand signals.

■ base hit (baseball)
a play in which the batter hits the ball in fair territory and reaches at least first base before being thrown out.

■ base line (baseball)
the white chalk lines that extend from home plate through first and third base to the outfield and up the foul poles, inside which a batted ball is in fair territory

and outside of which it is in foul territory.

■ **base on balls (baseball)**
walk; four balls and the hitter advances to first base.

■ **base position (badminton)**
an area in the centre of the court where a single's player usually wants to be positioned after each shot.

■ **baseball (baseball)**
the baseball's core is made of rubber and cork. Yarn is wound around the rubber and cork centre. Then 2 strips of white cowhide are sewn around the ball. Official baseballs must weigh 5 to 5 1/4 ounces and be 9 to 9 1/4 inches around.

■ **baseline (basketball)**
see *end line.*

■ **baseline (lawn tennis)**
a line at the end of the court, parallel to the netthat marks the lengthwise boundary of the playing area.

■ **baseline game (lawn tennis)**
a playing style in which the player hits almost all of his or her shots from near the baseline, rather than taking the net.

■ **baseline judge (lawn tennis)**
an official, stationed on a line with the baseline, who is responsible for determining whether shots are in or out. The baseline judges are seated on the same side of the court as the umpire.

■ **baseline player (lawn tennis)**
a player who practices the baseline game.

■ **bases empty (baseball)**
no runner on the bases.

■ **bases loaded (baseball)**
runners at each base.

■ **basket (basketball)**
attached to the backboard, it consists of a metal rim 18 in. diameter suspended 10' from the floor, from which a 15-18 corded net hangsand through which points are scored; also used to refer to a successful field goal.

■ **bat (badminton)**
a common name for the racket.

■ **bat (baseball)**
instrument used by the hitter while batting. In the ABL bats made of aluminium or wood. The bat must be no longer than 42 inches and no wider then 2 3/4 inches. Players are allowed to cover the first 8 inches of the bat's handle so they can grip it better.

■ **bat-and-pad catch (cricket)**
a hit that hits a batter's leg (pad) and is caught by a fielder before it touches the ground. A clear out.

■ **batter (baseball)**
an offensive player who takes his position in the batter's box.

■ **batter's box (baseball)**
an area marked by white chalk lines on the left and right side of home plate in which a player must stand while batting.

■ **battery (baseball)**
term referring to the pitcher and catcher combination.

■ **batting average (cricket)**
the average number of earned runs scored by a batter, defined as total runs scored divided by number of times the batter was out.

■ **batting order (baseball)**
the offensive line-up of a team that lists the player will bat. The batting order is given to the umpire before each game.

■ **baudry point (fencing)**
a safety collar placed around a live epee point to prevent dangerous penetration.

■ **bayonet (fencing)**
a type of electrical connector for foil and sabre.

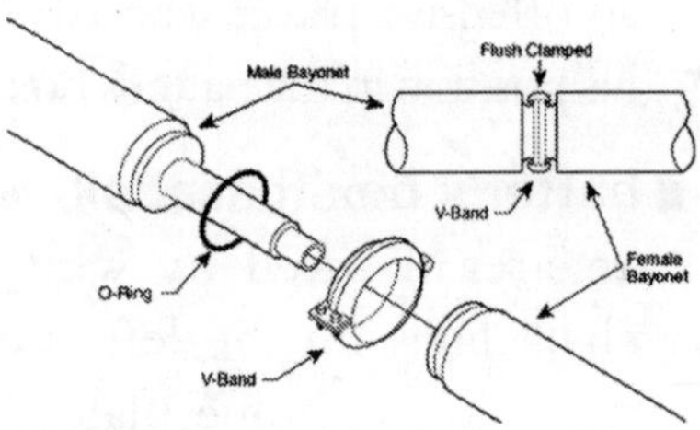

■ **beat (fencing)**
an attempt to knock the opponent's blade aside or out of line by using one's foible or middle against the opponent's foible.

■ **beat the defender (basketball)**
when an offensive player, with or without the ball, is able to get past an opponent who is guarding him.

■ **beat the defense (icehockey)**
to get by one or both of the defensemen.

■ **beat the goalie (icehockey)**
to outwit the goalie and score a goal.

■ **beat (football)**
when a player gets past an opponent trying to block or tackle him.

■ **behind the net (icehockey)**
the area of ice behind the goal cage is legal territory.

■ **biff (cycling)**
a crash.

■ **bind (fencing)**
an action in which the opponent's blade is forced into the diagonally opposite line.

■ **binding (rugby)**
the method by which players grip one another to form a maul, ruckor scrum. A player must bind with at least one arm on a teammate.

■ **bird (badminton)**
the shuttlecock.

■ **bit (equestrian)**
the metal mouthpiece to which the reins are attached.

■ **black card (fencing)**
used to indicate the most serious offences in a fencing competition. The offending fencer is usually expelled from the event or tournament.

■ **blackout (football)**
when a regional network TV affiliate is forbidden from showing a local game because it is not sold out.

■ **blade (field hockey)**
the flat side of the stick's head, which is used for hitting the ball.

■ **blade (rowing)**
the part of an oar that pushes against the water.

■ **blade (table tennis)**
the paddle without its rubber surface.

■ **blind pass (basketball)**
a pass from a ball handler who does not see his receiver, but is estimating where he should be.

■ **blind pass (icehockey)**
to pass the puck without looking.

■ **blinders (equestrian)**
same as blinkers.

■ **blindside (rugby)**
same as weakside.

■ **blinkers (equestrian)**
flaps on the bridle that keep a horse from seeing to the side or back.

■ **blitz (football)**
a play where the defensive team sends players rushing towards the line of scrimmage as soon as the ball is snapped to try to sack the quarterback.

■ **block (badminton)**
a shot, usually from near the net, on which the racket is not swung, but simply used as a backboard to return the shuttlecock.

■ **block (cycling)**
to disrupt a chase by slowing down the pace line. It can be the action of one or more riders. Blocking is often done to protect a teammate who's in the lead.

■ **block (lawn tennis)**
to return the ball by holding the racket stationary rather than swinging it.

■ **block (table tennis)**
a return shot on which the paddle is simply held in front of the ball, with little or no movement.

■ **blocked shot (basketball)**
the successful deflection of a shot by touching part of the ball on its way to the basket, thereby preventing a field goal.

■ **blocking (basketball)**
the use of a defender's body position to illegally prevent an opponent's advance; the opposite of charging.

■ **blocking (rugby)**
see *obstruction.*

■ **blocking (football)**
the act of preventing a defensive player from getting to the ball carrier; blockers use their arms and bodies but may not hold an opponent.

■ **blue lines (icehockey)**
two blue, 12-inch wide lines running parallel across the ice, each 60 feet from the goal; they divide the rink into three zones called the attacking, defending and neutral (or center) zones; defending blue line is the line closer to a player's own net; attacking blue line is the one farther from his net; used in determining offsides.

■ **bo (martial arts)**
a fighting staff, about 6 feet long and 1 inch in diameter, made of polished wood and used in several martial arts.

■ boarding or board-checking (icehockey)
a minor penalty which occurs when a player uses any method (body checking, elbowing or tripping) to throw an opponent violently into the boards; if an injury is caused, it becomes a major penalty.

■ boards or board wall (icehockey)
a wooden or fiberglass wall 3 1/2 to 4 feet high which surrounds the rink to keep the puck and players from accidentally leaving the rink and injuring spectators; all rinks have shatterproof glass that rises above the boards to provide additional protection.

■ body check (icehockey)
when a hockey player bumps or slams into an opponent with either his hip or shoulder (the only legal moves) to block his progress or throw him off-balance; it is only allowed against an opponent in control of the puck or against the last player to control it.

■ body lock (wrestling)
a hold in which a wrestler locks his arms around the opponent's body and takes him to the mat.

■ body throw (wrestling)
a move in which a wrestler locks his arms around the opponent's body and throws him to the mat.

■ body weight (weightlifting)
each athlete is weighed, to the nearest 10 grams, two hours before competition begins. If two lifters have exactly the same total, the one with the lower body weight is given the higher ranking.

■ bokken (martial arts)
a wooden swordoriginally used by samurai in place of a real sword during practice,

now a weapon in its own right.

■ **bomb (weightlifting)**
to fail making a good lift in either or both of the two lifts, which results in no score. Also bomb out.

■ **bomb (football)**
a long pass thrown to a receiver sprinting down the field.

■ **bonk (cycling)**
a state of exhaustion brought on by lack of food during a long stretch of riding.

■ **boosters (basketball)**
alumni supporters of college teams.

■ **boot (rowing)**
a device that holds the bow of a boat until the starting signal, when it drops below the water.

■ **bottom position (wrestling)**
in par terre, the wrestler who is on hands and knees is in the bottom position.

■ **bout (fencing)**
an assault at which the score is kept.

■ **bout (wrestling)**
a match between two wrestlers, which is made up of two periods of three minutes each. A bout ends before the regulation time in the event of a fall, a technical fall, an injury defaultor a disqualification. If the bout is tied or neither wrestler has three points after time expires, there is an overtime period.

■ **bow (rowing)**
the forward part of a boat.

■ **bowball (rowing)**
a round rubber protrusion attached to the bow of a shell for protection.

■ **bowl game (football)**
a college football game played in late-December or

early-January, after the regular season, between two successful teams.

■ **bowled (cricket)**
an out which is achieved by a pitch that hits the batter's sticks, whether or not touched by the bat. Rather like baseball's strike-out.

■ **bowling average (cricket)**
the (average) number of earned runs scored off a pitcher/bowler per every out he takes.

■ **bowman (rowing)**
the oarsman, who sits nearest the bow.

■ **bowside (rowing)**
the left side of the shell, from the point of view of the oarsmen, who face the stern. By extension, the oarsmen whose oars are in the water on that side.

■ **box score (baseball)**
the progression of the game as written in a series of boxes indicating hits, runs, errors and player substitutions of each inning played.

■ **boxing out (basketball)**
a player's attempt to position his body between his opponents and the basket to get rebounds and prevent the opponents from doing so.

■ **break (basketball)**
see *fast break*.

■ **break (cricket)**
a change in direction of a pitch, after it is bounced by the pitcher.

■ **break (icehockey)**
a chance to start a rush when the opposing forwards are caught out of position.

■ **break (lawn tennis)**
to win a game as receiver; as a noun, a synonym for service break.

break back (lawn tennis)
to win a game as receiver immediately after having suffered a service break.

break point (lawn tennis)
a point which will result in a service break if it's won by the receiver.

break-away (cycling)
the action of a rider or group of riders that launches an attack and leaves the main group behind.

breakaway (icehockey)
a fast break in which an attacker with the puck skates in alone on the goalie, having gotten past or clear of the defensemen, trapping the opponents behind the play.

breakaway (rugby)
see *flanker*.

breakdown (wrestling)
the act of getting an opponent to the mat on his stomach or side.

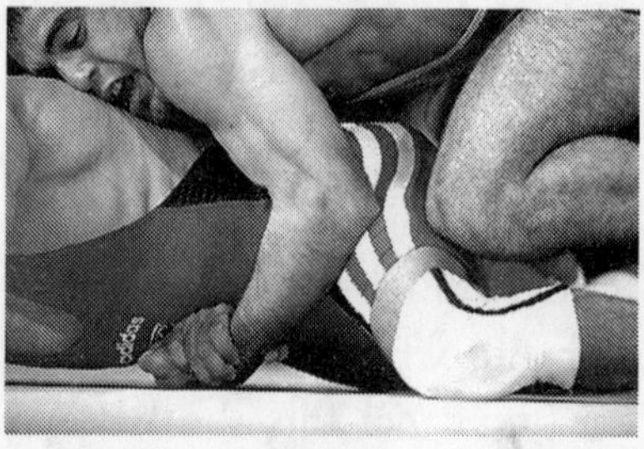

break-fall (martial arts)
a technique that lessens the impact of a fall.

breaking ball (baseball)
an off-speed pitch that curves.

breaking pass (icehockey)
a pass to a teammate who is trying for a breakaway.

breeches (equestrian)
tight-fitting trousers that don't cover the entire leg, worn for riding.

■ **bridge (cycling)**
to move from one group of riders to another group that's farther ahead.

■ **bridge (wrestling)**
an arched position adopted by a wrestler, with his back above the mat, usually to avoid being pinned but sometimes as an offensive move.

■ **bridge out (wrestling)**
an escape move in which a wrestler rolls from a bridge onto the stomach.

■ **bridle (equestrian)**
a harness of leather straps that fits around the horse's head and holds the bit.

■ **broadsword (fencing)**
any sword intended for cutting instead of thrusting; sabre.

■ **broken time (fencing)**
a sudden change in the tempo of one fencer's actions, used to fool the opponent into responding at the wrong time.

■ **brutality (water polo)**
an exclusion foul called for very rough play, such as punching or kicking an opponent or official.

■ **bucket rig (rowing)**
an arrangement on an eight or a four so that Riggers 2 and 3 are on the same side of the boat.

■ **bujutsu (martial arts)**
fighting arts of Japan's ancient warrior class.

■ **bullpen (baseball)**
area designated for pitchers to warm-up. Generally consists of two mounds and two home plates.

■ **bully (field hockey)**
a method of starting or restarting play, similar to the face-off in ice hockey. The referee places the ball on the ground between two opposing players. They tap the flat sides of their sticks together

three times and then go for the ball.

■ **bump-and-run (football)**
a technique used by pass defenders, where they hit a receiver once within 5 yards (1 yard in college) of the line of scrimmage to slow him down and then follow him to prevent him from catching a pass.

■ **bumper (cricket)**
a ball that is bounced high enough to hit a batter's head or shoulders; cricket's equivalent of the beanball.

■ **bunny (water polo)**
a goal scored on a hard shot close to the goalkeeper's head. Also called a donut.

■ **bunny-hop (cycling)**
jumping the bike over an obstacle without dismounting.

■ **bunt (baseball)**
short hit that is executed by letting the ball hit the bat (not swinging). Used to surprise the fielders or to advance a runner.

■ **bushido (martial arts)**
the code of ethics practiced by the bushi and samurai class in ancient Japan; the Japanese for way of the warrior.

■ **butt-ending (icehockey)**
a major penalty which occurs when a player jabs an opponent with the shaft of his hockey stick.

■ **button (fencing)**
the safety tip on the end of practice and sporting swords.

■ **button (rowing)**
a collar on the shaft of the oar that keeps it from slipping through the oarlock. It can be adjusted up or down to increase or decrease the rower's leverage.

■ **bye (lawn tennis)**
the right to advance to the next round of a tournament without playing a match. Top-seeded players are often given byes in the first round. See *seed.*

■ **bye (s) (cricket)**
run (s) scored on wild pitches. i.e. when the ball goes past the wicket-keeper/ catcher without having been touched by the batter and runs can be scored (much like stolen bases on wild piches in baseball). The runs are added to the team total as extras, but not credited to batters. nor charged to bowlers.

■ **cadence (cycling)**
pedaling rate, in revolutions per minute of one of the cyclist's feet.

■ **cadence (rowing)**
the beat at which the oarsmen are rowing. With coxed crews, the coxswain often raps out the cadence to keep the oarsmen pulling together.

■ **call a play (football)**
instruct players to execute a pre-planned play.

■ **called game (baseball)**
a game suspended or ended by the umpire.

■ **campbell conference (icehockey)**
was one of the two conferences in the NHL that contained the Norris and Smythe Divisions until 1992-93; renamed the Western Conference in 1993.

■ **canter (equestrian)**
a gait in which three legs are simultaneously off the ground. It's faster than a trot but slower than a gallop.

■ **canvas (rowing)**
the tapered section of a boat between the bowman and the bow of the boat or between the coxswain and the stern. So called because it used to be covered with canvas.

■ **cap (rugby)**
the honour of playing for a national team against another national team. If a player has appeared in five such games, he or she is said to have five caps.

■ **cap (water polo)**
each player wears a cap, numbered 1 to 13, with the goalkeeper wearing No. 1. Team caps are of contrasting colors, typically white for one team and blue for the other. Goalkeepers wear red caps.

■ **captain (rugby)**
the player in charge of a team during a match.

■ **carbon blade (table tennis)**
a blade with a layer of carbon between two wood surfaces.

■ **carom (icehockey)**
a rebound of the puck off the boards or any other object.

■ **carry (badminton)**
the illegal act of catching the shuttlecock on the racket and then slinging rather than striking it. Also called sling or throw.

■ **carry (lawn tennis)**
an illegal shot, on which the ball is ball is held and/or carried on the racket, rather being struck.

■ **cartwheel (gymnastics)**
a move in which the hands are placed on the mat or apparatus to one side of the body, one after the other, with the legs following.

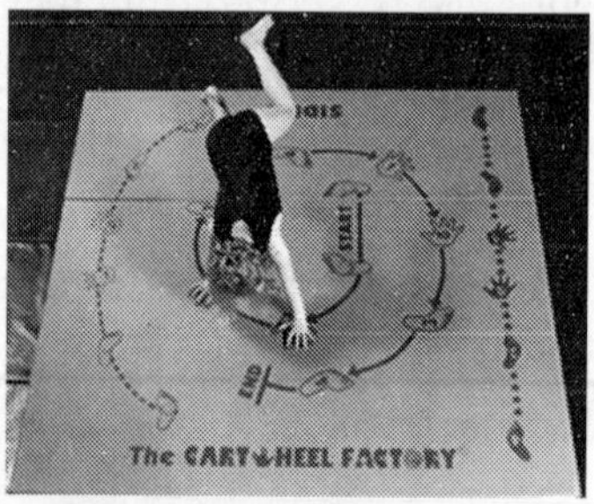

■ **catch (rowing)**
the portion of the stroke when the oar initially engages the water.

■ catch a crab (rowing)
to make a a faulty stroke, usually because the blade enters the water at an angle, instead of perpendicularly.

■ catch as catch can (wrestling)
another name for freestyle or folkstyle.

■ catcher (baseball)
player positioned behind home plate and responsible for receiving the pitch from the pitcher.

■ catcher's box (baseball)
area behind home plate in which the catcher must stand until the pitcher delivers the ball.

■ caught (out) (cricket)
an out resulting from a hit caught by a fielder in the air, i.e. before touching the ground, like baseball's pop fly.

■ centre (rugby)
one of two backs, an inside centre (usually No. 12) and an outside centre (usually No. 13).

■ centre circle (basketball)
the circular area at midcourt from which jump balls are taken.

■ centre court (lawn tennis)
the main court at a tennis arena, where the championship and other major matches are played.

■ center face-off circle (icehockey)
a circle, measuring 30 feet in diameter, at the centre of the ice where the puck is dropped in a face-off to start the game and to restart the game after a goal has been scored.

■ centre ice (icehockey)
the area between the two blue lines, also called the neutral zone.

■ centre line (field hockey)
the line that divides the field into two halves.D:

■ centre line (icehockey)
a red, 12-inch wide line across the ice midway between the two goals.

■ centre line (table tennis)
a white line down the middle of the table, parallel with the side lines that divides the courts into half-courts.

■ centre line judge (lawn tennis)
an official who is responsible for watching the centre service line to determine whether a serve has entered the service court.

■ centre mark (field hockey)
a spot in the middle of the pitch where the ball is placed for a bully.

■ centre mark (lawn tennis)
a line, 2 inches wide and 14 inches long that marks the midpoint of the baseline.

■ centre or centre forward (icehockey)
the centre player in the forward line who usually leads his team's attack when they are trying to score a goal; he takes part in most of the face-offs; he controls the puck and tries to score or pass it to a teammate who is in a better position to score a goal.

■ centre pass (field hockey)
a pass from the centre of the field, used to start a half or following a goal. The player must pass the ball to a teammate who is at least 1 metre back. Also known as the pass back or push back.

■ centre service line (lawn tennis)
a line, extending from the net to the midpoint of the service line, which marks the boundary for both service courts.

■ centre-back (water polo)
a defensive player whose main job is to cover the opposition's center-forward.

■ centre-forward (water polo)
a team's chief attacking player, who is usually positioned directly in front of the opponent's goal between the two-meter and four-meter lines. Also called the hole man, hole setor two-meter man.

■ centreing pass (icehockey)
a pass from an attacking player towards the middle of the ice to a teammate with a better angle at the goal.

■ central circle (wrestling)
the inner circle, 1 metre in diameter, on the wrestling mat.

■ central wrestling area (wrestling)
a circle, 8 metres in diameter, inside the passivity zone.

■ chainsuck (cycling)
the unhappy situation when the chain gets caught between the rear wheel and chain stay.

■ chair (lawn tennis)
the umpire's seat and, by extension, the umpire, as in The chair ruled that the shot was out.

■ chalk (weightlifting)
magnesium carbonate powder that lifters put on their hands to improve the grip.

■ change of engagement (fencing)
engagement of the opponent's blade in the opposite line.

■ change up (baseball)
a slow-pitch thrown with the exact arm action as a fastball, designed to disrupt the timing of the hitter.

■ changeover (lawn tennis)
a 90-second period after every odd-numbered game in a set, when players change sides.

■ charge down (rugby)
blocking a kick by the opponent.

■ charging (basketball)
an offensive foul which occurs when an offensive player runs into a defender who has established position.

■ charging (icehockey)
a minor penalty which occurs when a player makes a deliberate move of more than two steps when body checking an opponent; if serious injury is caused or blood is drawn it becomes a major penalty.

■ chase (cycling)
the pursuit, usually by a group of riders, of another group that's farther ahead, often one engaged in a breakaway.

■ chasers (cycling)
riders who are involved in a chase.

■ check (rowing)
deceleration caused by poor rowing technique, usually because an oarsman puts pressure on the stretcher without applying simultaneous, countervailing pressure on the pin.

■ check it down (rowing)
an emergency command from the coxswain to jam oars into the water in order to stop the boat.

■ check or checking (icehockey)
any contact initiated by a defending player against an opponent to get the puck away from him or slow him down; there are two main types of checks (icehockey) stick check and body check; these are only allowed against a player in control of the puck or against the last player to control it immediately after he gives it up; checking after too many steps or strides becomes charging.

■ **checked swing (baseball)**

a partial swing. If the swing has gone more than halfway around, the umpire can rule it a full swing or strike.

■ **chief referee (weightlifting)**

see *referee.*

■ **chinaman (cricket)**

a left-hander's googly i.e., a pitch that looks as if it could break into a right-handed batter on the bounce, but breaks away instead. So called because the first person to have delivered such a pitch was of Chinese extraction, in the West Indies !

■ **chip (lawn tennis)**

a soft shot, hit with backspinthat just drops over the net; as a verb, to hit such a shot. It's similar to the drop shot, but is more commonly used against an opponent who is at the net, forcing a difficult volley.

■ **chip (rugby)**

same as *pop kick.*

■ **choke-up (baseball)**

gripping the bat up on the handle away from the knob of the bat.

■ **chop (lawn tennis)**

a shot hit with a sharp, downward chopping motion, resulting in a great deal of backspin.

■ **chop (table tennis)**

a sharp downward stroke that produces backspin.

■ **chopper (rowing)**

see *hatchet.*

■ **chopper (table tennis)**

a player, who hits a lot of chops.

■ **chui (martial arts)**

a violation that gives the opponent a yuko. If given to a

combatant who already has a chui, the chui is increased to keikoku (Judo).

■ **circuit (cycling)**

one trip over a course that is traversed more than once during a road race; the equivalent of a lap in track acracing.

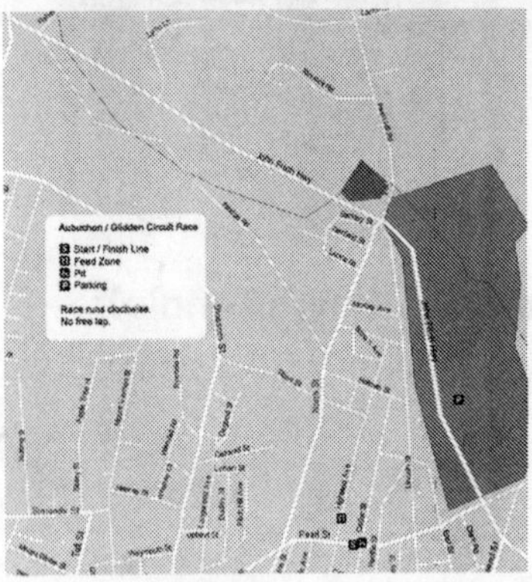

■ **circuit race (cycling)**

a multi-lap race on a course of two miles or longer.

■ **classification points (wrestling)**

in a tournament, wrestlers are awarded classification points for each bout won. The points are used to determine seedings in the final round. The following table is used:

outcome Score
victory by fall 5 points
technical fall 4 points
injury default 4 points
disqualification 4 points
decision 3 points

the loser of a match by decision or technical superiority wins 1 point of he or she accumulated any technical points during the bout. In the case of an overtime period, the winner and the loser both receive the same number of classification points as the number of technical points in the bout.

■ **clean and jerk (weightlifting)**

a two-part lift in which the weight must first be pulled from the platform to the shoulders in one motion while splitting or squatting and then standing up (the clean). Before the bar begins to descend, the lifter must jerk the weight overhead with a quick movement, ending with the arms fully extended and the body completely upright.

■ clean round (equestrian)
a round that's completed without a single fault or penalty.

■ clean winner (lawn tennis)
a shot that cannot be reached by the opponent.

■ clean-up hitter (baseball)
player who hits fourth in the batting order.

■ clear (badminton)
a shot, similar to the lob in tennisthat is hit over the opponent's head, usually to a point near the back boundary line. The attacking clear is an attempt to score, while the high clear is a defensive shot.

■ clear (field hockey)
to move the ball away from the goal after an attack by the other team has been stopped.

■ clear hip circle (gymnastics)
a hip circle in which the hips do not touch the bar.

■ clear out (basketball)
see *one-on-one showdown.*

■ clearing the puck (icehockey)
getting the puck out of one's own defensive zone.

■ clearing the zone (icehockey)
when a defending player sends the puck out of the opponent's attacking zone, all the attacking players must leave or clear the zone to avoid being called offsides when the puck reenters the zone.

■ cleat (cycling)
a metal or plastic attachment on the sole of the cycling shoe that fits into an opening to fasten the shoe to the pedal.

cleaver (rowing)
see *hatchet.*

clipping (football)
blocking an opponent below the waist from behind; this illegal block is a personal foul, punishable by a 15-yard penalty.

closed grip (lawn tennis)
a grip in which the racket face is tilted downward, toward the court.

closed paddle (table tennis)
a paddle tilted downward, toward the table. Striking the ball with a closed paddle tends to produce topspin.

closed racket (lawn tennis)
a racket held with a closed grip.

closer (baseball)
relief pitcher who specialises in pitching the last few outs of a game. General used to hold a lead in the late innings of a game.

collar (weightlifting)
a metal attachment that encircles the bar at each end to hold the discs in place.

combination (equestrian)
a series of jumps set within a stride or two of each other.

combination paddle (table tennis)
a paddle that has two different coverings on opposing sides of the face, for example, anti-spin rubber on one side and sticky rubber on the other .

commanding the blade (fencing)
grabbing the opponent's blade with the off-hand, illegal in sport fencing.

Commissioner (basketball)
the president of the NBA.

■ **complete game (baseball)**
statistical credit to a starting pitcher for pitching the entire game.

■ **complete pass (football)**
a forward pass to a teammate who catches it in the air.

■ **composition (gymnastics)**
the overall arrangement of individual movements and skills into a gymnastics routine.

■ **compound (fencing)**
also composed; an action executed in two or more movements; an attack or riposte incorporating one or more feints.

■ **compulsories (gymnastics)**
routines that contain movements required of all gymnasts. Compare optionals.

■ **conferences (football)**
groups into which teams are divided in professional and college football; the NFL is divided into National and American Conferences.

■ **control (wrestling)**
a wrestler who has a dominant position that restricts the opponent's mobility is said to be in control.

■ **control of the ball (water polo)**
when not touching it, a player is considered in control of the ball if it is on the water in front of the horizontal plane of his or her shoulders.

■ **controlling the game clock (football)**
the use of tactics by an offensive team to either save or use up time on the game clock, which often dictates its choice of plays.

■ **conversation (fencing)**
the back-and-forth play of the blades in a fencing match, composed of phrases (phrases d'armes) punctu-

ated by gaps of no blade action.

■ **conversion (rugby)**

A kick at the goal posts, after a try has been awarded that scores 2 points. It can be a dropkick or a placekick. If a placekick, the opponents can rush as soon as the kicker moves toward the ball, but a dropkick can't be rushed. The kick is taken from a spot perpendicular to where the try was awarded.

■ **corner throw (water polo)**

a free throw awarded to the attacking team if a defensive player touched the ball last before it went out over the goal line. It's taken from the two-meter line on the side nearest the spot where the ball went out of bounds.

■ **corps-a-corps (fencing)**

lit. body-to-body; physical contact between the two fencers during a bout, illegal in foil and sabre.

■ **coule' (fencing)**

also graze, glise'or glissade; an attack or feint that slides along the opponent's blade.

■ **count (baseball)**

the number of called balls and strikes on a hitter.

■ **counter-attack (fencing)**

an offensive action made against the right-of-way or in response to the opponent's attack.

■ **counter-disengage (fencing)**

a disengage in the opposite direction, to deceive the counter-parry.

■ **counter-drive (table tennis)**

an attacking shot used to return the opponent's attacking shot.

■ counter-parry (fencing)
a parry made in the opposite line to the attack; ie. the defender first comes around to the opposite side of the opponent's blade.

■ counter-riposte (fencing)
an attack that follows a parry of the opponent's riposte.

■ counter-time (fencing)
an attack that responds to the opponent's counter-attack, typically a riposte following the parry of the counter-attack.

■ country (cricket)
old name for the outfield, in cricket.

■ coup lance' (fencing)
a launched hit; an attack that starts before a stop in play but lands after. Valid for normal halts, but not valid at end of time.

■ coupe' (fencing)
also cut-over; an attack or deception that passes around the opponent's tip.

■ course (rowing)
a straight area in the water, typically 4 to 8 lanes wide, for rowing competition. The standard Olympic course is 2,000 meters long.

■ court (badminton)
the badminton court is 17 by 44 feet for singles, 20 by 44 feet for doubles. There is a short service line, 6 feet and 6 inches from the net, on each side of the courtthat marks the beginning of the service court. A long service line, 2 feet and 6 inches from each backline, marks the end of the service court.

■ court (basketball)
the 94' x 50' area bounded by 2 sidelines and 2 end lines containing a basket at each end, on which a basketball game is played.

■ court (lawn tennis)
the tennis court is 78 feet long and 27 feet wide for singles, 36 feet wide for doubles. It is divided across the middle by the net. Service lines are marked 21 feet

from each side of the net and parallel to it. The area bounded by the singles sidelines and the service line is divided into two equal parts, the service courts, by the centre service line, which is halfway between the sidelines and parallel to them.

■ court (table tennis)

the playing area on one side of the net, which is 5 feet wide and 4 ½ feet long. Sometimes used to mean the entire surface of the table.

■ court tennis (lawn tennis)

the ancestor of modern tennis, court tennis apparently developed during the Middle Ages in monastery courtyards and then moved into the courtyards of castles, where it was played by kings and nobles. It has a very complicated scoring system, which has been somewhat simplified for modern lawn tennis. Also known as real tennis, in which real is the Spanish word for royal.

■ court vision (basketball)

a player's ability to see everything on the court during play — such as where his teammates and defenders are set up — which enables him to make better choices in passing; the best point guards possess this.

■ cover (field hockey)

to position oneself between an opposing player and the ball. The goal circle, so called because it's shaped like a D.

■ cover (icehockey)

when a player stays close to an opponent to prevent him from receiving a pass or making a play on offense.

■ cover drive (cricket)

a drive that is hit away from the batter's body, in baseball's first-base direction.

■ cover or coverage (football)
preventing a player from gaining yards; in pass coverage, a defender follows a receiver to prevent him from catching a pass; in kick coverage, members of the kicking team try to prevent a long kick return.

■ cox (rowing)
short for coxswain.

■ cox box (rowing)
a small electronic device that amplifies the coxswain's voice and also gives a readout of information, such as the current stroke rating.

■ coxed (rowing)
descriptive of a boat or crew that has a coxswain.

■ coxless (rowing)
descriptive of a boat or crew with no coxswain.

■ coxswain (rowing)
the helmsman, who has two important jobs: To keep the boat moving straight by making minor corrections to the rudderand to keep the oarsmen rowing at the desired stroke rate.

■ cradle (wrestling)
a hold in which one arm is around the neck of the opponent, the other around the neck, with the hands gripped tightly together.

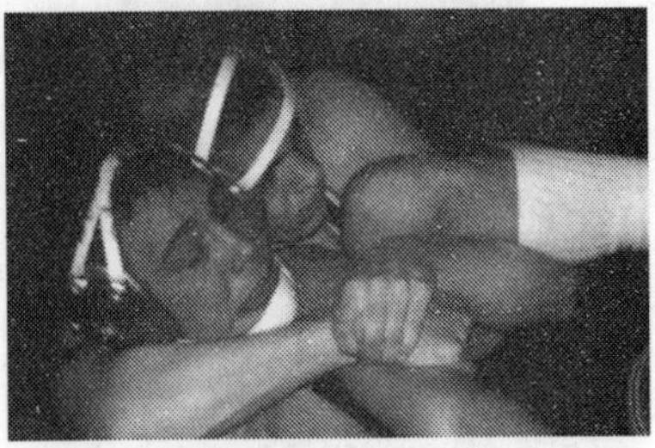

■ crease lines (icehockey)
the red lines that form the semi-circular area with a 6-foot radius in front of the goal called the goal crease.

■ criterium (cycling)
a multi-lap race on a course of a mile or less.

■ croise (fencing)
also semi-bind; an action in which the opponent's blade is forced into the high or low line on the same side.

■ crop (equestrian)
a short whip.

■ cross (fencing)

an advance or retreat by crossing one leg over the other; also passe' avant (forward cross), passe' arriere (backwards cross).

■ cross bar (icehockey)

the horizontal bar that connects the top of the two goalposts.

■ cross country (equestrian)

riding that simulates a ride through open country, including various types of jumps.

■ cross (gymnastics)

a skill performed on the still rings, in a straight body or L position, with the body perpendicular to the floor and the arms stretched perpendicular to the body. See also *inverted cross.*

■ cross-bar (rugby)

the horizontal bar between the goal posts, which is 3 meters (9 feet, 10 inches) above the ground.

■ cross-checking (icehockey)

a minor penalty which occurs when a player holds his stick in both hands and drives the shaft into an opponent; a stick check where a player has both hands on the stick and no part of the stick on the ice; if serious injury is caused or blood is drawn it becomes a major penalty and a game misconduct.

■ cross-country (cycling)

descriptive of a mountain bike race that takes place over trails, jeep roadsand similar difficult terrain.

■ cross-court (lawn tennis)

descriptive of a shot that is hit from one side of the court to the other, as well as over the net. For example, the player hits from the right-hand side of the back court to the right-hand side of the opponent's backcourt.

■ **cross-face (wrestling)**
a hold in which the wrestler's forearm is pressed across the opponent's face.

■ **crossover dribble (basketball)**
when a ball handler dribbles the ball across his body from one hand to the other.

■ **crotch lift (wrestling)**
a hold in which the arms are wrapped around the opponent's upper thigh, often used to turn the opponent over for a pin.

■ **cup (equestrian)**
an attachment on the wing of a jump that holds the rail.

■ **cup (table tennis)**
to close the palm on the ball when tossing it up for a serve. Cupping is against the rules, since it can be used to put spin on the ball.

■ **curve (baseball)**
pitch that moves down, across or down and across, depending upon the rotation of the ball.

■ **cut (fencing)**
an attack made with a chopping motion of the blade, normally landing with the edge.

■ **cut (lawn tennis)**
to hit the ball with a short, downward slicing motion, often drawing the racket strings across it to give some sideways spin in addition to backspin.

■ **cut back (football)**
a sudden change in direction taken by a to make it more difficult for defenders to follow and tackle him.

■ **cutter, leg- or off- (cricket)**
a fast pitch where a slashing arm action rather than wrist or finger spin is used to get a

slight break off the bounce.depending on the direction of the break, it can be called a leg-cutter or off-cutter.

■ **cylinder (basketball)**
the imaginary area directly above the basket where goal tending or basket interference can occur.

■ **daisy cutter (lawn tennis)**
a low shot that skids or takes a very low bounce, usually because of backspin.

■ **dan (martial arts)**
the Korean word for degree, usually used as a suffix with a number prefix to indicate a practitioner's rank, as in shodan. First dan is the lowest degree and 10th dan is the highest.

■ **danger position (wrestling)**
a position in which a wrestler's back is at less than a right angle to the mat.

■ **dangerous play (field hockey)**
an action that could result in injury to any player, including the player performing the action. It includes an illegal tackle, a raised ball and playing the ball while lying on the ground.

■ **dead ball (basketball)**
any ball that is not live; occurs after each successful field goal or free-throw attempt, after any official's whistle or if the ball leaves the court; it stops play which is then resumed by a jump ball, throw-in or free-throw.

■ **dead ball (rugby)**
the ball becomes dead if it goes out of bounds or if the referee stops play for any reason.

■ **dead ball (table tennis)**
a ball that has little or no spin.

■ **dead ball (football)**
a ball becomes dead when a play is over and becomes live as soon as it is snapped for the next play.

■ dead puck (icehockey)
a puck that flies out of the rink or that a player has caught in his hand.

■ dead time (water polo)
the time when the ball is dead, between the whistle for a foul and the restarting of play and the clock. Compare *live time.*

■ dead-ball line (rugby)
one of two lines marking the lengthwise boundaries of the field, located at the back of the in-goal area, a maximum of 22 meters from the try-line.

■ dead-time foul (water polo)
any foul that's committed during dead time.

■ deception (fencing)
avoidance of an attempt to engage the blades; see *disengage.*

■ decision (wrestling)
a victory in which the winner leads the opponent by 1 to 9 points. Compare technical fall.

■ deck (rowing)
one of the sections of a shell near the bow and stern that are covered, usually with thin plastic or fiberglass.

■ declaration (cricket)
in unlimited-over games, a decision by the captain of a batting side to stop batting and put the other side in to bat usually done to allow enough time to win a game.

■ default (lawn tennis)
the failure or refusal of a player to take part in or complete a match, resulting in a victory for the opponent. Also used as a verb, as in Smith was forced to default because of a knee injury.

■ **default (wrestling)**
a win declared because of the opponent's disqualification or injury.

■ **defender (table tennis)**
a player who concentrates on returning shots, hitting many pushes, chops and blocks, waiting for the opponent to make a mistake. Compare *attacker*.

■ **defense (basketball)**
the act of preventing the offense from scoring.

■ **defensemen (icehockey)**
two players who make up a team's defensive unit usually stationed in or near their defensive zone to help the goalie guard against attack; sometimes they lead an attack. The left defenseman covers the left half of the rink, the right defenseman plays to the right, but they can skate into each other's territory.

■ **defensive line (icehockey)**
consists of two defensemen.

■ **defensive lob (lawn tennis)**
a high shot, often used against an opponent at or near the net, designed to buy time.

■ **defensive rebound (basketball)**
a rebound of an opponent's missed shot.

■ **defensive team (water polo)**
the team that does not have control of the ball; opposite of attacking team.

■ **defensive volley (lawn tennis)**
a volley, usually hit from below the top of the net, simply as a means of returning the opponent's shot to keep a rally going. See *offensive volley*.

■ **defensive zone (icehockey)**
the zone or area nearest a team's goal (the goal they are defending).

■ **deflection (icehockey)**
causing any pass or shot to stray from its intended course; a shot or pass that hits some object such as a stick or skate and goes into the net for a score or when a goalie hits the puck away.

■ **deke or deking (icehockey)**
a decoying or faking motion by the puck-carrier; the art of making a defensive player think you are going to pass or move in a certain direction when you are not. There are shoulder dekes, stick dekes and head dekes.

■ **delay of game (icehockey)**
a minor penalty imposed on any player, who purposely delays the game in any way, such as shooting or batting the puck outside the playing area or displacing the goalpost from its normal position.

■ **delayed penalty (icehockey)**
a penalty against a team that has only 4 players on the ice, assessed only when one of its players gets out of the penalty box.

■ **delayed whistle or delayed call (icehockey)**
when an official raises his arm but does not blow his whistle, waiting to see the outcome of a play before calling a penalty; this is done so as not to penalize the non-offending team by stopping its momentum.

■ **derailleur (cycling)**
a mechanism that moves the bicycle chain from one gear sprocket to another when the gear is shifted.

■ **derobement (fencing)**
deception of the attack.

■ **designated hitter (base-**

ball)
player who bats in the pitcher's spot in the line-up. The DH does not have a fielding position.

■ **deuce (lawn tennis)**
when players are tied at 40 (three points each), the score is called deuce. At deuce, a player must win two points in a row to win the game. If the players split the following two points, the score reverts to deuce.

■ **deuce (table tennis)**
the situation when the score is 10 all (20-all if game is 21). The players then alternate serves until one of them wins by taking a 2-point lead.

■ **deuce court (lawn tennis)**
the receiver's right service court, where he or she receives serve when the score is deuce. The opposite of advantage court.

■ **devil take the hindmost (cycling)**
a popular name for the miss-and-out race.

■ **diagonals (equestrian)**
movements that test the co-ordination of the rider's posting and up-down motion with the diagonal movement of the horse's legs while trotting.

■ **diamond (baseball)**
the infield playing surface.

■ **dig deep (rowing)**
to thrust an oar too deeply into the water, resulting in loss of power. Also knife in.

■ **dihue (martial arts)**
an assistant instructor.

■ **direct (fencing)**
a simple attack or riposte that finishes in the same line in which it was formed, with no feints out of that line.

■ **disc (weightlifting)**
One of the cylindrical weights that are loaded onto the bar-

bell. Discs come in eight weights and are color coded: 25 kilograms (red); 20 kg (blue); 15 kg (yellow); 10 kg (green); 5 kg (white); 2.5 kg (black); 1.25 kg (chrome); 0.5 kg (chrome); 0.25 kg (chrome).

■ **disengage (fencing)**
a circular movement of the blade that deceives the opponent's parry, removes the blades from engage mentor changes the line of engagement.

■ **disk wheel (cycling)**
a solid wheel, without spokes that's used in the time trial and sometimes in other races because of its aerodynamic qualities.

■ **dismount (gymnastics)**
to leave the apparatus as the finale of a routine, usually with a difficult twist.

■ **disobedience (equestrian)**
a term that covers several types of misbehavior, including deviating from the course, a refusal, run-outand resistance.

■ **displacement (fencing)**
moving the target to avoid an attack; dodging.

■ **disqualification (wrestling)**
a wrestler may be disqualified for brutality or un sportsman like conduct.

■ **division (football)**
in the NFL, sub-groups within conferences, such as the Eastern, Northern, Southern and Western Divisions; also, a grouping of teams in college football, where Division I contains the most competitive teams and Division III the least.

■ **do (martial arts)**
the path to self enlightenment. Literally, the way.

■ **dojang (martial arts)**
the Korean word for a training hall, a cognate of the Japanese dojo.

■ **dojo (martial arts)**
a hall in which martial arts are taught and practiced. Liter-

ally place of the way in Japanese.

■ **domestique (cycling)**
the team rider in a long race who's responsible for getting food, waterand other from the support vehicle and distributing them to his teammates.

■ **donut (water polo)**
same as *bunny*.

■ **donut (baseball)**
circular shaped weight that slides over the bat. The weight is used when a player is loosening up in the one deck circle.

■ **double (fencing)**
in epee, two attacks that arrive within 40-50 ms of each other.

■ **double' (fencing)**
an attack or riposte that describes a complete circle around the opponent's bladeand finishes in the opposite line.

■ **double (rowing)**
a sculling boat for two rowers.

■ **double back (gymnastics)**
two consecutive back flips.

■ **double century (cricket)**
an individual score of 200 runs or more by a batter.

■ **double coverage (football)**
when 2 defensive players cover one receiver.

■ **double fault (lawn tennis)**
the server is given two attempts at a valid serve. If both attempts fail, it is a double fault and the receiver wins the point. Also used as a verb.

■ **double foul (water polo)**
simultaneous fouls by players on opposing teams.

■ **double hit (lawn tennis)**
the act of striking the ball twice during a single stroke; it results in loss of the point.

■ **double hit (table tennis)**
a shot on which the ball contacts a player's paddle or

paddle hand twice; results in loss of point.

■ **double hole (water polo)**
descriptive of an of an offense that stations an attacker in front of each post of the goal; also known as double post.

■ **double minor (icehockey)**
a type of minor penalty given for certain accidental infractions that result in an injury to another player or for certain deliberate attempts to injure an opponent that are unsuccessful; penalty time of 4 minutes is served, double the time of a normal minor penalty.

■ **double play (baseball)**
any defensive play that results in two base runners being called out.

■ **double post (water polo)**
same as *double hole.*

■ **double team (basketball)**
when two teammates join efforts in guarding a single opponent.

■ **double twist (gymnastics)**
a single layout flip with two twists.

■ **double (baseball)**
a hit that enables a batter to reach second base.

■ **doubleheader (baseball)**
two games played back to back by the same teams.

■ **double-leg tackle (wrestling)**
a move in which a wrestler takes the opponent down by grasping both of the opponent's legs and pulling them.

■ **doubles (lawn tennis)**
a match between two teams of two players each.

■ **doubles (table tennis)**
a game between two teams of two players each. Partners have to alternate shots.

■ **doubles court (lawn tennis)**
the playing area for a doubles match, which includes the two alleys as well as the singles court. The area is 78 feet long by 36 feet wide.

■ **double-time (fencing)**
parry-riposte as two distinct actions.

■ **down signal (weightlifting)**
an indication from the chief referee that the lift has been completed and the lifter can drop the bar.

■ **down the field (football)**
in the direction of the opponent's goal line.

■ **down the line (lawn tennis)**
descriptive of a shot that is hit straight from near the sideline, as opposed to a cross-court shot.

■ **down (football)**
one of 4 chances a team on offense has to gain 10 yards; also, the state of a player who has just been tackled; also, a ball that a player touches to the ground in the end zone to get a touchback.

■ **downcourt or down the court (basketball)**
the direction a team on offense moves, from its backcourt into its frontcourt and towards its own basket.

■ **draft (basketball)**
the method by which NBA teams annually select college or foreign players to their teams, designed to promote balanced competition in the NBA.

■ **draft (cycling)**
to ride close behind another racer in order to take advan-

tage of decreased wind resistance.

■ draft choice (football)
a player chosen by a professional sports team from a pool of college players in an annual draft.

■ drag volley (lawn tennis)
a volley hit with backspin.

■ draw (cricket)
in an unlimited-overs game of one or two innings, a situation where neither side wins the first team's total is not surpassed, but the innings are not completed. (No draws are allowed in limited-over games).

■ draw (lawn tennis)
the process by which matches are arranged and scheduled for a tournament. Generally, seeded players are given byes or scheduled before the draw and names of the other entrants are then randomly selected to determine match-ups and order of play. The word is also used to mean the schedule itself, after the draw has been completed. See also *seed.*

■ draw (weightlifting)
the process of allocating random numbers to competitors, which determine the lifting order.

■ Dream Team (basketball)
the name given by the media to the U.S. basketball team that won the gold medal at the 1992 Barcelona Olympics; it was the first time non-amateurs were permitted to represent the country; the members of this team were Charles Barkley, Larry Bird, Clyde Drexler, Patrick Ewing, Magic Johnson, Michael Jordan, Christian Laettner, Karl Malone, Chris Mullin, Scottie Pippen, David Robinson and John Stockton. In the 1996 Olympics, the U.S. team was called Dream Team II and in 2000, Dream Team III.

■ dressage (equestrian)
a type of competition in which judges award points for the performance of the horse and rider in a series of movements testing the rider's control and the horse's training.

■ dribble (field hockey)
to control the ball with short strokes of the stick while on the move. Also used as a noun.

■ dribble (water polo)
to swim with the ball, usually while it rides on the wake in front of the swimmer.

■ dribble or dribbling (basketball)
when a player repeatedly pushes, pats, taps or bats the ball toward the floor with one hand to cause the ball to bounce back up to either of his hands; used to advance the ball or keep control of it.

■ dribble series (basketball)
a number of consecutive dribbles which end when a player allows the ball to rest in one or both hands; a player is only permitted one dribble series before he must pass or shoot.

■ drive (badminton)
a hard, low shot that travels almost horizontally.

■ drive (cricket)
a hit executed by the batter in which he swings the bat in a long arc, much like teeing off at golf and sends the ball in one of several possible directions.

■ drive (rowing)
the portion of a stroke, between the catch and the release, when the oar is forcefully moving through the water.

■ **drive (table tennis)**
a shot hit with great force, usually a loop.

■ **drive (water polo)**
a quick move to the area in front of the goal by an offensive player who does not have the ball. As a verb, to make such a move.

■ **drive to the basket (basketball)**
to move rapidly toward the basket with the ball.

■ **drive (football)**
the series of plays a team puts together in an attempt to score.

■ **drop (water polo)**
a defense in which players drop back to protect the centre of the pool and attempt to block passes and shots.

■ **drop back (football)**
when a quarterback, after taking the snap, takes a few steps backward into an area called the pocket to get ready to pass.

■ **drop goal (rugby)**
a drop kick at the posts, worth three points if successful.

■ **drop kick (rugby)**
a kick on which the ball is dropped to the ground and kicked just as it bounces.

■ **drop kick (football)**
a type of free kick where a player drops the ball and kicks it right after it hits the ground; rarely used today.

■ **drop pass (icehockey)**
when a player simply leaves the puck behind for a teammate following him to pick up.

■ **drop shot (badminton)**
a softly-hit shot that drops just over the net.

■ **drop shot (lawn tennis)**
a soft shot that drops just over the net; usually hit with backspin to minimise its bounce. It's most commonly used against an opponent who is playing deep, as contrasted with the chip shot.

■ **drop shot (table tennis)**
a shot that falls just over the net.

■ **drop volley (lawn tennis)**
a drop shot that's hit before the ball has bounced.

■ **drops (cycling)**
the lower portion of down-turned handlebars.

■ **dry (fencing)**
also steam; fencing without electric judging aids.

■ **dry pass (water polo)**
a pass that can be caught above the water.

■ **duck (cricket)**
a zero individual score, awarded to a batter who is out without scoring a single earned run.

■ **duck-under (wrestling)**
a takedown move in which the wrestler ducks under the opponent's arm to get behind him and then uses a lift, throw or trip to take the opponent to the mat.

■ **dugout (baseball)**
enclosed seating facility reserved for players, substitutes, coaches and other uniformed team members.

■ **dummy (rugby)**
a fake pass.

■ **dunk (basketball)**
when a player close to the basket jumps and strongly throws the ball down into it; an athletic, creative shot used to intimidate opponents.

■ **dynamic start (weightlifting)**
the preparatory movement of the hips that gives the lifter the momentum needed to position the body under the bar.

■ earned run (baseball)
a run scored on a hit, walk or steal, without benefit from a defensive error on the play.

■ eastern conference (icehockey)
the renamed Wales Conference beginning with the 1993-94 season which contains the Atlantic, Northeast and Southeast Divisions.

■ echelon (cycling)
a diagonal line of riders, in which each rider is downwind of the rider immediately ahead. It's a cooperative group, since each rider takes a turn in front, fighting the wind while the other riders are shielded from it.

■ economy rate (cricket)
the average number of earned runs scored off a pitcher/bowler per over that he bowls/pitches a measure of pitching efficiency.

■ eggbeater (water polo)
an alternating leg kick used to tread water and lift much of the torso out of the water.

■ eight (rowing)
a sweep-oar boat with eight rowers and a coxswain.

■ elbowing (basketball)
it is a violation if a player vigorously or excessively swings his clbows, even if there is no contact; it is a foul if contact is madeand an automatic ejection if that contact is above shoulder level.

■ elbowing (icehockey)
a minor penalty which occurs when a player strikes his opponent with an elbow to impede his progress.

■ eligible receiver (football)
a player allowed by the rules to catch a forward pass; all offensive players are eligible except linemen and the quarter-

back, who must notify the referee if they wish to become eligible and stand at least one yard behind the line of scrimmage before the snap.

■ empty-net goal (icehockey)
a goal scored against a team that has pulled the goalie.

■ en garde (fencing)
also On Guard; the fencing position; the stance that fencers assume when preparing to fence.

■ encho-sen (martial arts)
an extension of play to determine the winner of a tied match. (Karate).

■ encroachment (football)
if a player (besides the center) is in the neutral zone and contact occurs prior to the snap; a foul punishable by a 5-yard penalty.

■ end line (basketball)
the boundary line behind each basket; also called the baseline.

■ end line (table tennis)
one of the two white lines marking an end of the table.

■ end line (football)
the boundary line that runs the width of the field along each end.

■ end zone (football)
the area between the end line and goal line bounded by the sidelines, which a team on offense tries to enter to score a touchdown.

■ endboards (icehockey)
the boards at each end of the rink.

■ enforcer (icehockey)
also called the policeman; is usually the most penalised player on a team; he has the job of protecting his teammates from harm; generally a larger player who is not afraid of any fight.

■ engagement (fencing)
when the blades are in contact with each other, eg. during a parry.

■ envelopment (fencing)
an engagement that sweeps the opponent's blade through a full circle.

■ epee (fencing)
a fencing weapon with triangular cross-section blade and a large bell guard; also a light duelling sword of similar design, popular in the mid-19th century; epee de terrain; duelling sword.

■ ergometer (rowing)
a stationary rowing machine that allows indoor practice. Erg, for short.

■ error (lawn tennis)
a shot that fails to cross the net or lands out of the court, resulting in loss of the point. See forced error; unforced error.

■ error (baseball)
Defensive mistake that allows a batter to stay at the plate or reach first base or that advances a base runner.

■ escape (wrestling)
if an athlete gets out from being under control in the bottom position and gets to his feet, facing his rival, it is an escape, which scores one point.

■ established position (basketball)
when a defensive player has both feet firmly planted on the floor before an offensive player's head and shoulder get past him; the offensive player who runs into such a defender is charging.

■ exclusion area (water polo)
an area outside the field of play where a player must wait after an exclusion foul.

■ exclusion foul (water polo)
a foul that results in the offending player being sent to

the exclusion area for 20 seconds or until the opposing team has scored a goal. Exclusion fouls include: Interfering with a corner throw, free throw or goal throw; holding, pullingor sinking an opponent who is not holding the ball; intentionally kicking or striking an opponent; committing any act of brutality; and intentionally splashing water in an opponent's face. After an exclusion foul, the opposing team is awarded a free throw at the spot of the foul.

■ **execution (gymnastics)**
technical performance of a routine, including form, style and technique.

■ **exhibition game (icehockey)**
a game not included in the regular-season schedule and which does not count in the standings; the All-Star Game or other games generally played before the season begins.

■ **expansion (icehockey)**
the addition of teams to the NHL.

■ **expansion draft (icehockey)**
a special arrangement to assist new franchises in obtaining players, where expansion teams choose players from other teams' rosters.

■ **expansion team (icehockey)**
a team that has been recently added to the NHL.

■ **expedite system (table tennis)**
a method of limited a game's duration under certain circumstances, most commonly if neither player has reached 9 points after 10 minutes of play (19 points after 15 minutes if game is 21). Players alternate serving and the receiver is awarded a point for returning 13 successive shots.

■ **exposure (wrestling)**
turning an opponent's shoulders to the mat, thus exposing him to the possibility of a pin.

■ **extra point (s) (football)**
additional point (s) scored by a team after it has scored a touchdown, either by a point-after-touchdown (1 point) or a 2-point conversion (2 points).

■ **face (lawn tennis)**
the flat area of the racket formed by the strings and bounded by the frame.

■ **face mask (icehockey)**
the protective mask worn by the goalie.

■ **face off (water polo)**
see *neutral throw.*

■ **face-off (icehockey)**
the method of starting play; the dropping of the puck by the official between the sticks of two opposing players standing one stick length apart with stick blades flat on the ice; used to begin each period or to resume play when it has stopped for other reasons.

■ **face-off circles and spots (icehockey)**
the various circular spots on the ice where an official and two players will hold a face-off to begin or to resume the action of the game; there is one blue face-off circle and four red face-off spots located in the neutral zone; two red face-off circles are found at each end of the ice.

■ **fair catch (rugby)**
a player may make a fair catch by catching the ball cleanly from a kick by the opposing side and calling Mark! He must have at least one foot on the ground behind his side's 22-meter line or within the in-goal area. A free kick is usually awarded from the spot of the catch, at the referee's discretion.

■ **fair catch (football)**
when a kick returner decides only to catch a punt or kick-off and not advance it, protecting himself from being hit by an opponent; he signals for a fair catch by raising one hand in the air and waving it.

■ **fair territory (baseball)**
part of the playing field within and including the first base and third base lines, from home base to the bottom of the playing field fence and perpendicular upwards. All foul lines are in the fair territory.

■ **fake or feint (basketball)**
a deceptive move to throw a defender off balance and allow an offensive player to shoot or receive a pass; players use their eyes, head or any other part of the body to trick an opponent.

■ **fall (equestrian)**
if the horse's shoulders or hindquarters or any part of the rider's body touches the ground, it is considered a fall, which brings automatic disqualification.

■ **fall (wrestling)**
when both of the opponent's shoulders are in contact with the mat (a pin), a wrestler is awarded a fall, which wins the match in international wrestling. In college wrestling, the pin must be held for one second, in high school wrestling for two seconds.

■ **falling on the puck (icehockey)**
a minor penalty, which occurs when a player other than

the goalie closes his hand on the puck, deliberately falls on the puckor gathers the puck under his body while lying on the ice.

■ false (fencing)
an action that is intended to fail, but draw a predicted reaction from the opponent; also, the back edge of a sabre blade.

■ false start (rowing)
a premature start by one or more boats.

■ fandori (martial arts)
free sparring using throws and takedowns.

■ fast ball (baseball)
a straight pitch thrown by the pitcher as hard as possible.

■ fast break (basketball)
also called the run-and-shoot offense, it begins with a defensive rebound by a player who immediately sends an outlet pass toward midcourt to his waiting teammates; these teammates can sprint to their basket and quickly shoot before enough opponents catch up to stop them.

■ fault (badminton)
any violation of the playing rules.

■ fault (lawn tennis)
an invalid service attempt. It is a fault if the serve fails to land in the receiver's service court; if the server swings and misses the ball entirely; or if the serve is made from beyond the baseline or from the wrong side of the centre mark. See also *double fault; foot fault; serve.*

■ faults (equestrian)
penalty points added to a score. The most common penalties are: first disobedience: 3 faults second disobedience: 6 faults third disobe-

dience: elimination obstacle knocked down: 4 faults one or both feet in the water: 4 faults fall of the horse or rider: elimination.

■ **faults include: (badminton)**
an illegal service, e.g., one that is done underhand or that does not land in the proper service court the shuttlecock hits the ground before it is returned a shot lands outside the boundaries, fails to go over the netor goes through the net a player hits the shuttlecock before it crosses the netor is guilty of a carry a player strikes the shuttlecock twice or both players on the same doubles team strike it.

■ **feather (rowing)**
to turn the blade of an oar while rowing so that it's parallel to the surface of the water. The blade should be feathered during release to minimise air resistance.

■ **feed (rugby)**
the act of rolling the ball into the scrum by the scrumhalf.

■ **feeding (icehockey)**
passing the puck.

■ **feint (fencing)**
an attack into one line with the intention of switching to another line before the attack is completed.

■ **fence (equestrian)**
a vertical obstacle. In show jumping, the maximum height is 1.6 meters and the fence is often made of materials such as hedges, fake stone, brick, planks and poles. In the three-day event, the fence is usually less than 1.2 meters high and it's made of natural materials that fit into the terrain.

■ **fencing time (fencing)**
the time required to complete a single, simple fencing action.

■ FIE (fencing)
Federation Internationale d'Escrime, the world governing body of fencing.

■ field (cycling)
the main group of riders in a race.

■ field (water polo)
the water polo field is 20 to 30 meters between the goal lines and 10 to 20 meters wide. There are white buoys on each side of the pool to indicate the goal lines and the half-distance line. At each end of the pool, there are colored buoys denoting the 2-meter lines (red), 4-meter lines (yellow)and 7-meter lines (green). Water depth is a minimum of 1.8 meters, but 2 meters is the preferred depth. The playing area extends a minimum of .3 meters behind the goal lines at each end of the pool. See also goal.

■ field goal (basketball)
when the ball enters the basket from above during play; worth 2 points or 3 points if the shooter was standing behind the 3-point line.

■ field goal (football)
a place kick that passes above the crossbar and between the uprights of the goalpost, earning the team that kicked it 3 points.

■ field player (water polo)
any player except a goalkeeper.

■ field position (football)
the location of a team on the field relative to the two goal lines; good field position for a team is near its opponent's goal line, while bad field position is close to its own goal line.

■ field sprint (cycling)
a sprint among riders in the main group, usually at the end of a stage in a long race.

■ fielder's choice (baseball)
term used when a fielder can chose among base runners or throw or tag out.

■ fifteen (lawn tennis)
the first point of a game for either player or side.

■ fifteens (rugby)
the most commonly played form of rugby, with 15 players on a side and two halves of 40 minutes each.

■ fighting (icehockey)
a major penalty which occurs when two or more players drop their sticks and gloves and fight; if a referee deems one player to be the instigator that player also receives a minor penalty and a misconduct penalty; the minor penalty for a less severe pushing and shoving match is called roughing.

■ figure eight (equestrian)
an exercise in which the horse traces two connected circles, one clockwise and one counter-clockwise.

■ fin (rowing)
the skeg.

■ Final Four (basketball)
the 4 regional champions (West, East, Midwest and Southeast) remaining from the 64 college teams that compete in the annual NCAA Tournament; they play one another to determine the national champion.

■ Finals, NBA (basketball)
the annual championship series of the NBA's post-season.

■ finish (rowing)
the final portion of the drive, just before the oar is taken out of the water.

■ finta in tempo (fencing)
a feint of counter-attack that draws a counter-time parry, which is decieved; a compound counter-attack.

■ fireman's carry (wrestling)

a takedown move in which the wrestler brings the opponent temporarily over his shoulders, then to the mat.

■ first 5/8th (rugby)

another name for the flyhalf.

■ first down (football)

the first chance out of 4 that a team on offense has to advance 10 yards down the field; as soon as it gains those yards, it earns a new first down.

■ first flight (lawn tennis)

the flight of the ball after it leaves the racket and before it bounces.

■ five-ball attack (table tennis)

a strategy in which the server attempts to win the point on the fifth ball over the net. The ideal sequence is serve, return, loop, return and kill.

■ fixation (weightlifting)

the act of holding the bar overhead with the arms straight and fully extended.

■ fixed gear (cycling)

a direct drive system, used on track bikes, in which the chain ring and rear cog are linked, so that the pedals turn constantly while the bicycle is moving and coasting isn't possible.

■ fixture (rugby)

another name for a rugby match.

■ flagrant foul (basketball)

unnecessary or excessive contact against an opponent.

■ flanker (rugby)

one of two forwards, who usually wear No. 6 and 7. The flanker binds on the outside of the scrum. Also known as wing forward or breakaway.

■ **flat (lawn tennis)**
descriptive of a low, fast, straight shot without spin.

■ **flat pass (icehockey)**
when a player passes the puck to a teammate along the surface of the ice.

■ **fleche (fencing)**
lit. arrow; an attack in which the aggress or leaps off his leading foot, attempts to make the hitand then passes the opponent at a run.

■ **flic-flac (gymnastics)**
a move very similar to the back handspring. The take-off is from one or both feet, with a backward jump onto the hands and a landing on the feet, in the standing position.

■ **flick (badminton)**
a deceptive shot, apparently soft, but transformed into a faster shot by quick wrist and forearm rotation.

■ **flick (fencing)**
a cut-like action that lands with the point, often involving some whip of the foible of the blade to throw the point around a block or other obstruction.

■ **flick (field hockey)**
to raise the ball from the ground into the air with a quick movement of the stick. The ball must not rise more than 18 inches above the playing surface. Also used as a noun.

■ **flip (table tennis)**
a soft shot hit with a quick upward turn of the wrist that imparts topspin, often used to return a soft serve that has backspin.

■ **flip pass (icehockey)**
a pass by a player to a teammate that lifts the puck from the ice and sends it through the air, usually for the pur-

pose of getting it over an opponent's stick.

■ **flip shot (icehockey)**
a shot in which a player cups the puck in his stick, then flips it with his wrists up off the ice towards the goal; this sometimes makes the puck harder to block.

■ **floor (basketball)**
the area of the court within the end lines and sidelines.

■ **floor exercise (gymnastics)**
an event in which the gymnast performs tumbling and acrobatic passes on a mat 40 feet square. The women's floor exercise is done to music.

■ **floor violation (basketball)**
a player's action that violates the rules but does not prevent an opponent's movement or cause him harm; penalised by a change in possession.

■ **florentine (fencing)**
an antiquated fencing style where a secondary weapon or other instrument is used in the off hand.

■ **fly ball (baseball)**
batted ball that goes high in the air in flights.

■ **flyaway (gymnastics)**
a dismount from a bar in which the gymnast swings down and lets go to do a flip backwards before landing.

■ **flyer (cycling)**
a surprise attack by a single rider.

■ **flyhalf (rugby)**
the back, usually No. 10, who calls plays for the back row and normally receives the ball from the scrumhalf. Also known as the outhalf, outside half or 1st 5/8th.

■ **flying change (equestrian)**
a manoeuver in the canter in which the horses changes its lead leg at every fourth, third, second and then single stride, resulting in a skipping movement.

■ **flying parry or riposte (fencing)**
a parry with a backwards glide and riposte by cutover.

■ foible (fencing)
the upper, weak part of the blade.

■ foil (fencing)
a fencing weapon with rectangular cross-section blade and a small bell guard; any sword that has been buttoned to render it less dangerous for practice.

■ folkstyle (wrestling)
a style of wrestling generally used in high schools and colleges, which is similar to freestyle wrestling but with more emphasis on control and safety.

■ follow on (cricket)
in a full two-innings game, where the team batting second is asked to bat again because its first innings total is far behind that of the other team.

■ follow through (lawn tennis)
the motion of the arm and racket after the ball has been struck.

■ foot fault (lawn tennis)
usually a fault caused by the server's foot entering the court before the racket contacts the ball. It is also a foot fault if any part of the server's foot is on the wrong side of the centre markor the server is walking or running while delivering the serve.

■ foot fault judge (lawn tennis)
an official responsible for calling foot faults. The foot fault judge is positioned on a line with the baseline, on the opposite side of the court from the baseline judge.

■ foot stretcher (rowing)
see *stretcher*.

■ force out (baseball)
an out created when a runner is forced to advance be-

cause there is another runner behind them, although they will be thrown or tagged out. The defensive player needs only to touch the base being approached by the runner with the ball in hand to record the out.

■ **force the pace (cycling)**
to increase speed in order to make the entire group go faster.

■ **forced error (lawn tennis)**
an error resulting from a good shot by the opponent. See *error; unforced error.*

■ **forcing shot (lawn tennis)**
a shot that puts the opponent on the defensive; often an approach shot.

■ **forecheck (icehockey)**
to check or harass an opponent who has the puck in his defensive zone and keep the opponents in their end of the rink while trying to regain control of the puck; usually done by the forwards.

■ **forecourt (badminton)**
the front third of the court.

■ **forecourt (lawn tennis)**
the area between the net and the service line.

■ **forefoot (equestrian)**
one of a horse's front feet.

■ **forehand (icehockey)**
a shot or pass taken from the right side of a right-handed player or from the left side of a left-handed player.

■ **forehand (lawn tennis)**
a shot hit from the racket side of the player's body; the right side for a right-hander.

■ **forehand (table tennis)**
a shot hit on the same side of the body as the paddle hand; the right side, for a right-handed player.

■ **forkball (baseball)**
a pitch thrown by placing the ball between the first two fingers, usually resulting in a sinking ball.

■ forte (fencing)
the lower, strong part of the blade.

■ forty (lawn tennis)
the third point of a game for either player or side. If both reach forty, it is called deuce.

■ forward (field hockey)
a player positioned in the offensive end of the field, whose chief job is to score. Also called an attacker.

■ forward (rugby)
one of a group of eight players, usually Nos. 1 through 8, who bind together in scrums, line up for lineouts and are in most rucks and mauls.

■ forward line or attacking line (icehockey)
consists of two wings (right and left) and a center; these three players play nearer the opponent's goal and are responsible for most of the scoring.

■ forward pass (rugby)
a pass that goes to a player who's ahead of the ball; illegal in rugby.

■ forward pass (football)
a pass thrown by a team closer to the opponent's goal line; a team is allowed to throw only one forward pass per play and it must be thrown from behind the team's line of scrimmage.

■ forward progress (football)
the location to which a ball carrier has advanced the ball, even if he was pushed backwards after getting there.

■ forward somersault (gymnastics)
a body roll on the floor exercise or balance beam, done forward with knees in the tuck position.

■ forwards (basketball)
the 2 players on the court for a team who are usually

smaller than the centre and bigger than the guards; often a team's highest scorers.

■ **forwards (icehockey)**
the three players who make up the attacking line or forward line of a team — the centre and the right and left wings.

■ **foul (basketball)**
actions by players which break the rules but are not floor violations; penalised by a change in possession or free-throw opportunities.

■ **foul (icehockey)**
any infraction of the rules that will draw a penalty.

■ **foul (rugby)**
among the fouls in rugby are: Striking, hacking, kickingor tripping an opponent; making a dangerous tackle; wilfully charging, obstructingor grabbing an opponent who doesn't have the ball; a deliberate knock-on or forward pass.

■ **foul ball (baseball)**
a ball that lands outside the first or third base foul lines.

■ **foul lane (basketball)**
the painted area 19' x 16' (12' in college) bordered by the end line and the foul line, outside which players must stand during a free-throw; also the area an offensive player cannot spend more than 3-seconds at a time in.

■ **foul line (basketball)**
the line 15' from the backboard and parallel to the end line from which players shoot free-throws.

■ **foul line (baseball)**
lines extending from home plate through 1st and 3rd base to the outfield fence and perpendicularly upwards. These lines are considered in play.

■ **foul territory (baseball)**
part of the playing field outside the first and third base lines extended to the fence and perpendicularly upwards.

■ **foul (football)**
a violation of football's rules by a team or player, punishable by a penalty.

■ **four (rowing)**
a sweep-oar boat for four rowers. There is competition for fours with coxswain and fours without coxswain.

■ **four or boundary (cricket)**
a line drive that reaches the fence, counting as four runs.

■ **four-metre foul (water polo)**
a foul by a defensive player inside the four-meter line directly aimed at preventing a goal. The opposing team is awarded a penalty throw.

■ **four-metre line (water polo)**
an imaginary line extending across the pool, four meters from each goal line.

■ **frame (lawn tennis)**
the oval portion of the racket that contains the strings; an unstrung racket.

■ **franchise (basketball)**
a professional team.

■ **franchise (icehockey)**
a team; the legal arrangement that establishes ownership of a team.

■ **franchise player (basketball)**
a star player around which a franchise is built.

■ **franchise (football)**
a team; the legal arrangement that establishes ownership of a team.

■ **free agent (football)**
a player whose contract with his most recent team has expired, allowing him to sign a new contract with any team that makes him an offer.

■ **free agent, restricted (basketball)**
an NBA player whose contract has expired and who has received a qualifying offer from his current club

which provides a salary level predetermined by the collective bargaining agreement. While this player is free to negotiate an offer from a new team, his current team has a right of first refusal to match that offer, thereby obligating him to remain with his current team.

■ **free agent, unrestricted (basketball)**
a player who has completed his 3rd NBA season (or 4th season, if his current team exercised its option to have him play for a 4th year) and is free to negotiate a contract with other NBA teams without his current team having a right of first refusal.

■ **free hit (field hockey)**
a play awarded for any infraction outside of the goal circle. It takes place at or near the spot of the infraction and all opposing players must stand at least five yards away.

■ **free kick (rugby)**
an uncontested kick, usually awarded for a minor penalty by the opponents. Except as a drop goal, a free kick cannot be taken directly at the goal posts.

■ **free kick (football)**
a type of kick taken to start or restart play after a team has scored, with no defenders nearer than 10 yards away; includes a kickoff and a kick after a safety.

■ **free throw (water polo)**
when play has to be restarted after the ball crosses a sideline or after a foul that does not result in a penalty throw, a free throw is used. The player awarded the free throw may throw the ball or drop it into the water and dribble it before passing. At least two players, from either side, must touch the ball before a goal can be scored.

■ **freestyle (wrestling)**
a style of wrestling in which the legs may be used to execute attacks and the

opponent's legs are a legitimate target for attack. Also known as catch as catch can.

■ **free-throw (basketball)**
an unguarded shot taken from the foul line by a player whose opponent committed a personal or technical foul; it is worth 1 point.

■ **free-throw line (basketball)**
see *foul line.*

■ **free-throw line extended (basketball)**
an imaginary line drawn from the free-throw line to the sideline to determine the location for certain throw-ins.

■ **freeze the puck (icehockey)**
to hold the puck against the boards with the skate or stick in order to stop play briefly or gain a face-off.

■ **french grip (fencing)**
a traditional hilt with a slightly curved grip and a large pommel.

■ **frig rig (rowing)**
see *tandem rig.*

■ **froissement (fencing)**
an attack that displaces the opponent's blade by a strong grazing action.

■ **front (water polo)**
to defend between the centre forward and the player with the ball.

■ **front giant (gymnastics)**
a giant that begins with the body moving forward.

■ **front handspring (gymnastics)**
a handspring that begins with a forward flip.

■ **front hip pullover (gymnastics)**
a mount for the uneven bars in which the body is sup-

ported by the hands and the hip rests on a bar.

■ **front pike somersault (gymnastics)**
a forward somersault done with the knees straight.

■ **front row (rugby)**
the combination of two props and the hooker at the front of a scrum.

■ **front somersault (gymnastics)**
same as *forward somersault.*

■ **front splash (rowing)**
the spray that's kicked up when the oar enters the water at the catch.

■ **front split (gymnastics)**
a split in which one leg is forward, the other back.

■ **front stop (rowing)**
a small block on the stern end of the slide, which holds the seat in place.

■ **front walkover (gymnastics)**
a move from the front split handstand position in which one foot is brought down in back, followed by the other foot.

■ **frontcourt (basketball)**
the area between the midcourt line and the end line closest to the offense's basket.

■ **full nelson (wrestling)**
a hold in which both of the wrestler's arms are passed under the opponent's armpits and both hands are on the back of the opponent's head; illegal in amateur wrestling. See also half nelson.

■ **full paddle (rowing)**
the highest level of power possible from an oarsman.

■ **full pressure (rowing)**
same as *full paddle.*

full strength (icehockey)
when a team has its full complement of 6 players on the ice.

full toss (cricket)
a pitch that reaches the batter without a bounce, like a baseball pitch.

full tuck (cycling)
the deep crouch used by cyclists for better aerodynamics.

full twisting double back (gymnastics)
a double back with a full twist on either of the flips.

fullback (field hockey)
a player positioned in the defensive end of the field. Also called a defender.

fullback (rugby)
the back, usually No. 15, who typically plays deep behind the back line and is responsible for covering downfield kicks by the opponents.

full-court press (basketball)
when defenders start guarding the offense in the backcourt.

fuller (fencing)
the groove that runs down a sword blade to reduce weight.

full-in, back-out (gymnastics)
a double salto with a full twist, the twist completed during the first salto.

fumble (football)
when a ball carrier loses possession by dropping the ball or having it knocked away before a play ends; the first player to regain possession of the loose ball is said to make the recovery and his team becomes the offense.

fusen gachi (martial arts)
a win by default. (Judo).

gain line (rugby)
an imaginary line across the field at the point where the ball became dead.

gait (equestrian)
the manner in which a horse goes, based on the sequence and rhythm of its foot movements.

■ **gallery (lawn tennis)**
the spectator area at the ends and sides of a court. By extension, the spectators, as in, The gallery really applauded that shot.

■ **gallop (equestrian)**
the horse's fastest gait, in which all four feet are off the ground simultaneously.

■ **game (field hockey)**
a field hockey is made up of two halves, each 35 minutes in major contests, with a half-time intermission of 5 to 10 minutes.

■ **game (lawn tennis)**
a contest in which one player or side serves throughout. The first contestant to take four points wins the game, but the margin of victory must be at least two points. Scoring follows the sequence, Fifteen-Thirty-Forty-Game. If both players or sides reach forty, it's called deuce.

■ **game (table tennis)**
a table tennis game ends when one player has scored at least 11 or 21 points and at least 2 more than the opposing player. International rules now call for an 11-point game, but the 21-point game is still often used in informal player. See deuce.

■ **game (water polo)**
a water polo game consists of four periods of 7 minutes each, with a 2-minute interval between periods. If the score is tied after the fourth period, there are two overtime periods of three minutes each, with a 1-minute interval. If the score is still tied, a penalty shootout is used to determine the outcome.

■ **game clock (basketball)**
shows how much time remains in each of the four 12-minute quarters of an NBA game or two 20-minute halves of a college game.

■ **game point (lawn tennis)**
a point that will end the game if it is won by the leading player or side.

■ **game-set (lawn tennis)**
part of an announcement that a player has won the decisive game in a set, as in, Game-set to Miss Jones.

■ **game-set-match (lawn tennis)**
part of an announcement that a player has won the decisive game in a match, as in, Game-set-match to Miss Jones.

■ **gap (cycling)**
the difference in time between individuals and/or groups of riders. As a verb, to increase the gap.

■ **garryowen (rugby)**
same as *up and under.*

■ **gate (equestrian)**
a high, narrow fence.

■ **gate (rowing)**
a bar across the oarlock that keeps the oar from popping out.

■ **gaylord (gymnastics)**
a high bar move that consists of a front giant into a one-and-one half front salto over the bar, followed by a regrasp. Named for U. S. gymnast Mitch Gaylord, who created it.

■ **German rig (rowing)**
the arrangement of an eight so that riggers 4 and 5 are on the same side while the others alternate port and starboard.

■ **get the jump (icehockey)**
to move fast and thereby get a good start on the opponents.

■ **gi (martial arts)**
the uniform worn while practicing martial arts.

■ **giant (gymnastics)**
a swing on the horizontal bar in which the fully-extended body rotates 360 degrees around the bar.

■ **gienger (gymnastics)**
a flyaway with a one-half twist, followed by a re-grasp of the bar. Named for German gymnast Eberhard Gienger, who created it.

■ **glide (cricket)**
a hit which is executed like a drive but is angled to go behind the batter on his off side.

■ **goal (field hockey)**
the field hockey goal is a net, 7 feet high, 12 feet wideand 4 feet deep.

■ **goal (icehockey)**
provides one point; scored when a puck goes between the goalposts from the stick of an attacking player and entirely crosses the red line between the goalposts; also the informal term used to refer to the area made of the goalposts and the net guarded by the goalie and into which a puck must enter to score a point.

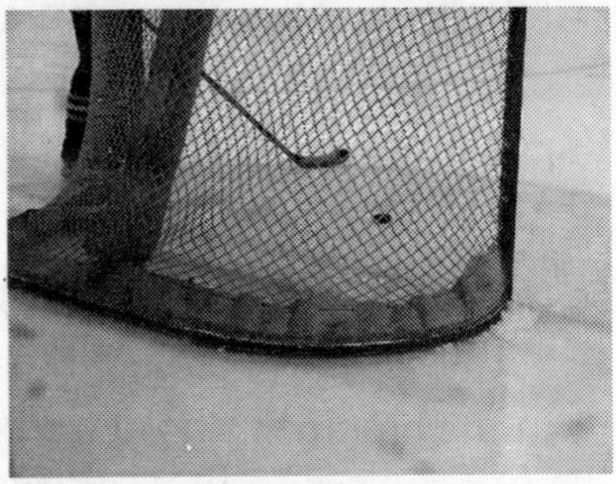

■ **goal (rugby)**
a score of 3 points awarded for drop-kicking the ball over the opponents goal-post during play or place-kicking it through on a penalty kick. The ball must pass between the goal posts and above the cross-bar.

■ **goal (water polo)**
1) The water polo goal is made of two goal posts and a crossbar, from which a net is suspended. The goal posts are 3 meters apart and the crossbar is .9 meters above the water surface. 2) A score, which is made by throwing or dribbling the ball so that it goes completely across the goal line, between the posts and under the crossbar.

■ goal cage (icehockey)
a 6 foot wide by 4 foot high tubular steel frame consisting of a cross bar and two goalposts to which a net is attached.

■ goal circle (field hockey)
actually a D-shaped area made up of two quarter-circles, measured 16 yards out from each goal post and joined by a short straight line. An attacking player must be within this area to score. Also known as the shooting circle or striking circle.

■ goal crease (icehockey)
a semi-circular area with a 6 foot radius in front of the opening of the goal; denotes the playing area of the goaltender within which attacking players must not obstruct his movement or vision.

■ goal judge (water polo)
there are two goal judges, one positioned on a side of the pool at each goal line. The goal judge's chief responsibility is to determine whether a goal has been scored and, if so, to signal the score by raising and crossing both arms.

■ goal line (icehockey)
the two-inch red line between the goalposts that stretches in both directions to the sideboards.

■ goal line (rugby)
see *try-line.*

■ goal line (water polo)
An imaginary line that extends across the pool at the mouth of the goal. The playing area extends at least .3 metre behind the goal line.

■ goal line (football)
a line drawn across the width of the field, 10 yards inside each end line, which a team must cross with the ball to score a touchdown.

■ goal posts (rugby)
the posts located at the centre of the goal line at each end of the field, 18 feet, 4 inches apart, connected by a cross-

bar 9 feet, 10 inches above the ground.

■ **goal throw (water polo)**
a throw taken by the defending goalkeeper from behind the two-meter line to restart play if an attacking player was the last to touch the ball before it went out over the goal line.

■ **goalkeeper (field hockey)**
each team must have a goalkeeper among its eleven players. The goalkeeper is allowed to use the kickers and leg guards, as well as the stick, to propel the ball. The hands may also be used to stop the ball, but not to grasp it.

■ **goalkeeper (water polo)**
each team has a goalkeeper, who must remain behind the half-distance line. The goalkeeper alone is allowed to stand or walk on the floor of the pool, to jump from the floor of the pool, to use both hands on the balland to punch the ball.

■ **goalkeeper, goalie or goaltender (icehockey)**
the heavily padded player who guards the goal; prevents opponents from scoring by stopping the puck any way he can.

■ **goalpost (football)**
a tall metallic structure that stands at the back of each end zone; consists of a crossbar and two uprights that extend upward from it, supported directly above the end line by a base; teams try to kick the ball above the crossbar and between the uprights to score a field goal or extra point.

■ **goalposts (icehockey)**
the metal bars that frame the area to which the net is attached which rests on the centre of the goal line and be-

tween which a puck must pass to score a goal.

■ going for it (football)
when a team facing a fourth down decides to try for a new first down instead of punting; if it fails, it loses possession of the ball.

■ good length or good-length delivery (cricket)
a pitch which bounces just outside the batter's maximum forward reach (i.e. 3 to 5 yards from the wickets, depending upon batter's height).these pitches are the hardest for a batter to hit, because he cannot decide whether to step forward anyway or if he should step back and give himself the maximum distance from the bounce, to see what the ball might be doing.

■ good lift (weightlifting)
a lift that has been correctly completed, as determined by at least two of the three referees.

■ googly (cricket)
a pitch which is thrown with baseball's screwball grip but reverse finger spin. to look like a leg-break that should move across and away from the batter, but actually moves in the opposite direction, i.e. into the batter like an off-break, after it bounces.

■ goshi waza (martial arts)
throws in which the hip is used as the pivot point.

■ goshin jitsu (martial arts)
techniques of self defense.

■ grand amplitude (wrestling)
descriptive of a throw in which a wrestler lifts the opponent completely off the mat, sweeps him through the air in a curveand brings him down in the danger position.

■ grand prix (equestrian)
the highest stage of dressage, which is used to determine world and Olympic champions.

■ grand prix freestyle (equestrian)
the third and final round of grand prix competition, a

six-minute routine of dressage movements to musical accompaniment, choreographed by the rider.

■ **grand slam (lawn tennis)**
there are four tournaments in the Grand Slam of tennis: The Australian, Frenchand U. S. Opens and England's Wimbledon championship. The phrase came from contract bridge by way of golf.

■ **grand slam (baseball)**
a home run that is hit with a runner on every base. This hit scores 4 runs.

■ **granny gear (cycling)**
the lowest gear on a mountain bike, used for very steep climbs.

■ **grapevine (wrestling)**
a hold in which a wrestler wraps a leg around one of the opponent's legs, often preparatory to a throw.

■ **Greco-Roman (wrestling)**
a style of wrestling in which the wrestler may not attack the opponent's legs nor use his own legs to execute attacks.

■ **green card (field hockey)**
a card issued by the referee as a warning for a minor rules violation.

■ **green light (baseball)**
signal from the coach to hit the next good pitch or a signal to a base runner that gives the runner the authority to decide when to attempt a steal.

■ **greenie (water polo)**
a quick shot taken by a player after receiving a pass near the goal. Originally guerrini.

■ **grip (table tennis)**
the way in which the paddle is held.

■ **grip (weightlifting)**
the way in which the bar is held.

■ grip width (weightlifting)
the distance between the hands on the bar.

■ ground ball (baseball)
a ball hit in the infield by the batter that bounces in the infield.

■ grounder (baseball)
a ground ball.

■ groundstroke (lawn tennis)
a shot hit from the back court or behind the baseline after the ball has bounced; the standard shot in tennis.

■ grubber (rugby)
a kick that bounces or rolls along the ground.

■ guard (fencing)
the metal cup or bow that protects the hand from being hit. Also, the defensive position assumed when not attacking.

■ guarding (basketball)
the act of following an opponent around the court to prevent him from getting close to the basket, taking an open shot or making easy an pass, while avoiding illegal contact.

■ guards (basketball)
the 2 players on each team who are the smallest on the court; they usually handle setting up plays and passing to teammates closer to the basket.

■ gut wrench (wrestling)
a moved used when the opponent is face down on the mat. The wrestler puts both arms around the opponent's mid-section, gripping as tightly as possible, then goes into the bridge position and rolls the opponent over his own torso onto the back.

■ hadaka jime (martial arts)
a choke hold with the naked arm.

■ hairpin shot (badminton)
a shot made from very close to the net on which the shuttle rises just over the net and drops quickly on the other side. Often used to return a drop shot.

■ hajimae (martial arts)
begin; a command.

■ **half century (cricket)**
an individual score of 50 runs or more by a batter.

■ **half court (lawn tennis)**
the area of the court in the vicinity of the service line.

■ **half nelson (wrestling)**
a hold in which the wrestler's arm is passed under the opponent's armpit and the hand is on the back of the opponent's head. See also full nelson.

■ **half pass (equestrian)**
a forward and sideways movement in the which the horse must cross its legs.

■ **half pirouette (equestrian)**
a rhythmic, half-circle turn with the inside hind foot as the pivot.

■ **half squat (weightlifting)**
a squat in which the knees are bent only slightly.

■ **half volley (lawn tennis)**
a shot on which the ball is struck just after it has hit the court. Also used as a verb.

■ **halfback (field hockey)**
see *midfielder.*

■ **halfback (rugby)**
see *scrumhalf.*

■ **half-court (table tennis)**
one side of a court, 4 ½ feet long by 2 ½ feet wide, representing one quarter of the table, delineated by the net and the centre line.

■ **half-court line (lawn tennis)**
another name for the centre service line.

■ **half-court or set offense (basketball)**
when a team takes the time to develop a play in its frontcourt, such as the give-and-go or a screening play; opposite of fast break.

■ **half-distance line (water polo)**
an imaginary line, marked by white buoys that divides the field of play into two equal ends.

■ half-in, half-out (gymnastics)
a double salto with a half twist on each salto.

■ halfway line (rugby)
the line that extends all the way across the field at its midpoint.

■ halt (equestrian)
stop; a command.

■ hammer (cycling)
to ride very hard, at the limit of one's capabilities.

■ hammered (cycling)
totally exhausted.

■ handicap (cycling)
a type of track race, very popular in Australia, in which the riders start from different points, based on past performance. The fastest riders, known as scratch men, start at the usual start line, while the outmarkers start at various positions up to 250 meters away, thus getting a head start.

■ handle (rowing)
the section of the oar gripped by the oarsman.

■ hand-off (football)
a running play where the quarterback hands the ball to a back.

■ handspring (gymnastics)
a move in which the gymnast springs off the hands with a strong push from the shoulders.

■ handstand (gymnastics)
a move in which the body is supported on both hands, with the arms straight and the body vertical.

■ hane goshi (martial arts)
a springing hip throw. (Mainly judo).

■ hang (weightlifting)
a position in which the bar is above the platform but below the knees.

■ hang on (cycling)
to maintain contact with a group of riders, but just barely.

■ hang time (football)
the length of time a punt is in the air.

■ hansoku mate (martial arts)
a very serious violation that gives the opponent an ippon, thereby ending the match. (Judo).

■ hantei (martial arts)
the judge's determination of the winner when a match is tied in points.

■ hara (martial arts)
a person's centre of mass, believed to be the origin of the ki. Literally, Japanese for abdomen.

■ hardbat (table tennis)
an older type of paddle, on which the rubber sheet is attached with the pips out.

■ hat trick (cricket)
getting three batters out in three successive pitches.so called because in the 17th century, a pitcher/bowler who accomplished the feat was rewarded by an immediate bonus, collected by passing a hat among gathered spectators.

■ hat trick (icehockey)
three or more goals scored by a player in one game.

■ hatchet (rowing)
an oar with a cleaver-shaped blade that has a larger surface area than on the standard oar.

■ head (lawn tennis)
the part of the racket comprising the frame and strings.

■ head deke (icehockey)
when a player drops his head as though moving one way and quickly moves in another to fake out the opponent.

■ headlock (wrestling)
a hold in which an arm is around the opponent's neck and the hands are locked together. The opponent's arm must be gathered into the hold to prevent accidental choking.

■ headset (cycling)
the part of the bicycle frame where the fork, stemand handlebar are fitted.

■ heat (rowing)
a race within a race, from which the top finishers advance to further rounds that will ultimately determine the winner.

■ heavy ball (lawn tennis)
a shot hit with topspin, which drops sharply.

■ Heisman Trophy (football)
an award presented annually by the Downtown Athletic Club of New York to the best college football player in the country.

■ high bar (gymnastics)
1) In the uneven bars, the higher of the two bars. 2) The horizontal bar.

■ high percentage shot (basketball)
a shot that is likely to go in the basket, such as a layup.

■ high post (basketball)
an imaginary area outside either side of the foul lane at the free-throw line extended.

■ high stick (field hockey)
raising the stick above shoulder level; a violation.

■ high-sticking (icehockey)
a minor penalty which occurs when a player carries his stick above the normal height of his opponent's shoulders and hits or menaces the opponent with it; if injury is caused it becomes a major penalty; if a referee determines that the raising of the stick was unintentional and no contact occurred, it is considered a team infraction and a face-

off is held in the offender's defensive zone.

■ **hiki wake (martial arts)**
a draw. (Judo and karate).

■ **hilt (fencing)**
the handle of a sword, consisting of guard, grip and pommel.

■ **hind foot (equestrian)**
one of a horse's back feet.

■ **hip circle (gymnastics)**
a move on the uneven bars in which the body circles the bar with the hips touching it.

■ **hira basami (martial arts)**
a strike in which the first knuckle of the first fingeror the area between the thumb and the first finger, is the striking surface. Literally tiger's mouth.

■ **hit (field hockey)**
a swinging movement of the stick toward the ball.

■ **hit and run (baseball)**
play-action situation in which the batter must swing at the pitch while the base runner attempts to steal the base.

■ **hit on the rise (lawn tennis)**
to play the ball before it has reached the highest point of its bounce.

■ **hit (baseball)**
a play in which the batter safely reaches a base after hitting the ball, without aid from a fielding error or fielder's choice.

■ **hold (water polo)**
to lift or carry the ball, place the hand over or under it or press it beneath the water.

■ **hold serve (lawn tennis)**
to win a game in which the player is serving.

■ **hold water (rowing)**
a command from a coxswain to the oarsmen to place their blades horizontally in the water to slow the shell quickly.

■ **holding (icehockey)**
a minor penalty which occurs when a player grabs and holds onto an opponent (or his stick) with his hands or

arms to impede the opponent's progress.

■ holding the puck (icehockey)
see *falling on the puck.*

■ holding (football)
a foul where a player impedes the movement of an opponent by grasping or hooking any part of his body or uniform; punishable by a penalty — 10 yards if against the offense, 5 yards (10 yards in college) plus a first down if against the defense.

■ hole guard (water polo)
the defensive player who takes a position in front of his or her own goal in order to guard the opposing centre forward.

■ hole man (water polo)
see *centre forward.*

■ home field advantage (football)
the benefit a team gets by playing games in the area where it is based, due to fan support, familiarity with its surroundings and the lack of required travel.

■ home game (football)
a game played in a team's own stadium.

■ home plate (baseball)
the fourth station to be reached by the runner. The offensive team is credited with one run every time a player safely crosses this base. A pitched ball must cross the plate when thrown by the pitchers to be credited as a strike on the batter.

■ home run (baseball)
a ball hit out of the playing field in fair territory. A home run scores the batter and any base runners.

■ home team (icehockey)
the team in whose arena the game is being played; the team wearing the lighter uniforms.

■ homologated (fencing)
certified for use in FIE competitions.

■ **hook (cricket)**

a hit that is executed by the batter swinging his bat around his body and following up with a complete body turn, usually pivoting on one foot.works best on a pitch that is moving away from the batter on his leg side.

■ **hook (cycling)**

to block a following rider by moving the back wheel to the side.

■ **hook (weightlifting)**

a grip in which the lifter wraps the thumbs around the bar with the index and second fingers on top of the thumbs.

■ **hook check (icehockey)**

a sweep of the stick low to the ice to take the puck from an opponent's stick.

■ **hooker (rugby)**

the forward who usually wears No. 2. The hooker is supported by the props in the scrum and is responsible for gaining possession of the ball by hooking or blocking it with a foot.

■ **hooking (icehockey)**

a minor penalty which occurs when a player attempts to impede the progress of another player by hooking any part of the opponent's body with the blade of his stick; an illegal use of one's stick.

■ **hooks (cycling)**

the curved portions of down-turned handlebars.

■ **hopper (lawn tennis)**

a container that holds large quantities of tennis balls.

■ **horizontal bar (gymnastics)**

1) A piece of apparatus, a metal bar 240 centimeters long and 2.8 centimetres in diametres, suspended 275 centimetres above the floor. 2) A men's event performed

on the apparatus. The routine is made up of swinging parts with no intervening stops, including at least one release move, which includes a release and a re-grasp.

■ hull (rowing)
the skin of a racing boat, which is usually made of carbon fibre, fibreglass, wood or some combination of these.

■ hunt seat (equestrian)
a category of horsemanship for English riders, based on riding across country and jumping, as in foxhunting.

■ hunting stock (equestrian)
a broad band worn around a dressage rider's neck as a substitute for a necktie or choker.

■ icing (icehockey)
a violation which occurs when the team in possession of the puck shoots it from behind the red centre line across the opponent's goal line into the end of the rink (but not into the goal) and a member of the opposing team touches it first; results in a face-off in the offender's defensive zone; a short-handed team cannot be called for icing.

■ impeding (water polo)
hindering the movement of an opposing player who does not have possession of the ball.

■ in (lawn tennis)
descriptive of a good shot that lands in the opponent's court.

■ in bounds (football)
the region of the field inside the sidelines and end lines.

■ in quartata (fencing)
a counter-attack made with a quarter turn to the inside, concealing the front but exposing the back.

■ in the paint (basketball)
being in the foul lane area which is painted a different colour.

■ in time (fencing)
at least one fencing time before the opposing action, es-

pecially with regards to a stop-hit.

■ **inboard (rowing)**
the distance from the end of the oar's handle to the portion of the button that touches the oarlock.

■ **inbounds (basketball)**
the area within the end lines and sidelines of the court; also the act of bringing the ball into this area by means of a throw-in.

■ **incidental contact (basketball)**
minor contact usually overlooked by officials.

■ **incomplete pass (football)**
a forward pass that touches the ground before being caught.

■ **indirect (fencing)**
a simple attack or riposte that finishes in the opposite line to which it was formed.

■ **individual pursuit (cycling)**
a type of race in which the two riders start on opposite sides of the track and chase each other for a distance ranging from 3,000 to 5,000 metres. If one rider catches up to the other, the race is over. If not, the rider with the fastest time wins.

■ **infield (baseball)**
area 90' square with the corners being the four bases.

■ **infielder (baseball)**
fielder who occupies a position in the infield. Most commonly refers to the first baseman, second baseman, third baseman and shortstop.

■ **in-goal (rugby)**
the area between the try-line and the dead-ball line.

■ **injury default (wrestling)**
a win rewarded to a wrestler when the opponent cannot continue to compete because of an injury. Worth four classification points.

■ **injury time (rugby)**
extra time added to the end of a half to compensate for time stoppage due to injuries.

injury time (wrestling)
a period during which a match is halted because one of the wrestlers is injured or bleeding. If the wrestler cannot continue within two minutes, the match ends with an injury default.

inner (field hockey)
a forward who plays in or near the centre of the field. See also wing.

inning (baseball)
a period of play. There are 9 innings in a regulation game, each team bats in an inning until they record 3 outs. The visiting team always bats in the top half (beginning) of an inning. If the home team has a higher total after their opponents bat in the top half of the last schedule inning, the bottom half of the inning is not played and the score is final. A tie at the end of regulation play forces extra innings. The game continues until an inning is complete and the visitors have a higher score or until the home team breaks the tie (then) they don't complete the 3 outs.

innings (cricket)
the total number of runs scored by a team during its time at bat.

innings victory (cricket)
in a full two-innings game, a victory where one team scores more runs in a single innings than its opponent does in two.

inside centre (rugby)
the back who usually wears No. 12.

inside hand (rowing)
the hand closest to the oarlock.

inside out (table tennis)
descriptive of a shot hit with sidespin so that it will curve and bounce away from the opponent.

inside shooting (basketball)
shots taken by a player near or under the basket.

■ **inside water (water polo)**
the position of an attacking player who is in front of a defender and moving toward the goal.

■ **insistence (fencing)**
forcing an attack through the parry.

■ **inswing (cricket)**
a pitch that moves into a batter in the air, like baseball's curve ball.

■ **intentional grounding (football)**
a foul called against a quarterback who purposely throws an incomplete forward pass solely to avoid a sack; cannot be called if the pass lands at or beyond the line of scrimmage.

■ **intentional walk (baseball)**
four balls thrown on purpose to a batter advancing the hitter to first base. Generally, executed when 1st base is empty to set-up a force play.

■ **interception (fencing)**
a counter-attack that intercepts and checks an indirect attack or other disengagement.

■ **interception (football)**
a pass caught in the air (picked off) by a defender whose team immediately gains possession of the ball and becomes the offense.

■ **interchange (field hockey)**
a temporary switch of positions by teammates.

■ **interference (icehockey)**
a penalty in hockey called when a player attempts to impede the motion of another player not in possession of the puck.

■ **intermission (icehockey)**
a fifteen-minute recess between each of the three periods of a hockey game.

■ **interval (cycling)**
to alternate between forcing the pace and resting, with the intention of wearing out other riders.

■ **inverted cross (gymnastics)**
a skill performed on the still rings, in an inverted handstand position, with the arms stretched out perpendicular to the body.

■ **inverted rubber (table tennis)**
a type of covering for the blade that has a smooth hitting surface on the outside and the surface with pips attached to the blade. It's called inverted because it's basically the same covering used on a hardbat, but upside down.

■ **invitation (fencing)**
a line that is intentionally left open to encourage the opponent to attack.

■ **ippon (martial arts)**
a full win. (Judo and karate).

■ **irimi nage (martial arts)**
an entering throw, in which the attacker's arm lifts the opponent's chin. Also known as the twenty-year throw.

■ **irons (equestrian)**
stirrups.

■ **it is not cricket (cricket)**
an expression meaning, any action that is deceptive, unfair or underhanded.i.e. contrary to the spirit in which cricket is supposed to be played.

■ **italian grip (fencing)**
a traditional hilt with finger rings and crossbar.

■ **Italian rig (rowing)**
the arrangement of an eight so that bow and stroke riggers are on the same side while the others alternate port and starboard.

■ **jab (field hockey)**
to poke continually at the ball in an attempt to make the attacking player lose possession.

■ **jam (lawn tennis)**
to hit the ball at or near the opponent's body, forcing an awkward or weak return.

■ **jitsu (martial arts)**
Japanese word for techniques.

■ **jo (martial arts)**
a fighting staff, 3 to 4 feet in length, used in several martial arts.

■ **ju (martial arts)**
the idea of giving way and using the opponent's momentum against him, rather than opposing force to force. Literally gentle in Japanese and the basis of both judo and ju-jitsu.

■ **judges (fencing)**
additional officials who assist the referee in detecting illegal or invalid actions, such as floor judges or hand judges.

■ **judo (martial arts)**
a Japanese martial art invented early in the 20th century by Kano Jigoro, based on older styles of ju-jitsu. It has been an Olympic sport since 1964. Japanese for gentle way.

■ **judogi (martial arts)**
the judo uniform, a baggy jacket off white or off-white material and loose trousers.

■ **judoka (martial arts)**
a practitioner of judo.

■ **ju-jitsu (martial arts)**
an old Japanese martial art, based primarily on the principle of ju. Literally, the gentle art in Japanese. Often spelled as one word.

■ **jump (cycling)**
a sudden burst of speed that usually becomes a sprint.

■ **jump (equestrian)**
any obstacle that the horse has to jump over and/or across.

■ **jump ball (basketball)**
2 opposing players jump for a ball an official tosses above and between them, to tap it to

their teammates and gain possession; used to start the game (tip-off) and all overtime periods and sometimes to restart play.

■ **jump smash (lawn tennis)**
a smash that is hit while the player is jumping into the air.

■ **jumper (rugby)**
1. A rugby jersey.
2. The player in a lineout who's responsible for jumping to catch or intercept a throw.

■ **jumping (equestrian)**
short for show jumping.

■ **jump-off (equestrian)**
an extra round to break a tie for first place after the final round of show jumping competition.

■ **junk rubber (table tennis)**
anti-spin rubber or long pips rubber.

■ **jury (fencing)**
the 4 officials who watch for hits in a dry fencing bout.

■ **jury (weightlifting)**
a group of five officials who watch the competition to ensure that all rules are complied with.

■ **kake (martial arts)**
application of a technique.

■ **kamae (martial arts)**
posture.

■ **kansetsu waza (martial arts)**
techniques of controlling the opponent's joints to throw, control immobilise him.

■ **kapo (martial arts)**
arts of healing.

■ **karate (martial arts)**
a modern Japanese martial art that developed from old Okinawan striking arts. Japanese for empty hand.

■ **kata (martial arts)**
formal exercises comprising a series of grappling or striking movements that imitate fighting situations.

■ **katsu (martial arts)**
methods of revival and resuscitation.

■ **keepaway game (basketball)**
a tactic used by the team that is leading near the end of the game to keep the ball from its opponents to prevent them from scoring while using up time off the game clock; also called freezing.

■ **keikoku (martial arts)**
a serious violation that gives the opponent a waza-ari. (Judo).

■ **keirin (cycling)**
a Japanese variation of the motorpace, with only one motorbike. Riders fight for position, attempting to get into the motorbike's slipstream in order to increase speed. Just before the last lap, the motorbike leaves the track and the riders sprint to the finish. In Japan, there's parimutuel betting on the keirin. Also spelled keiren.

■ **kempo (martial arts)**
the way of the fist.

■ **kendo (fencing)**
japanese fencing, with two-handed swords.

■ **kendo (martial arts)**
the Japanese art of fencing, which uses two types of wooden sword, the bokken and the shinai. The bokken is used primarily for practice, the shinai for full contact sparring.

■ **keosuke (martial arts)**
attention; a command.

■ **key or keyhole (basketball)**
the area at each end of the court consisting of the foul circle, foul lane and free-throw line; named for the shape it had years ago.

■ **ki (martial arts)**
life energy in Japanese. (The Chinese word is chi.) Martial arts practitioners are taught to focus their ki into their techniques.

■ **kick (cycling)**
a burst of speed near the finish line in an attempt to beat another rider or riders.

■ **kick serve (lawn tennis)**
a serve hit with a great deal of spin, causing it to change direction when it bounces.

■ **kicker (field hockey)**
protective equipment that covers the front and sides of the goalkeeper's shoes, allowing him or her to kick the ball.

■ **kick-off (rugby)**
a place kick taken from the centre of the field to begin a half.

■ **kickoff (football)**
when a player kicks a ball from a tee at his own 30-yard line (35 in college) to the opposing team, whose player tries to advance it the other way; used to start the game, the second half and overtimeand to restart play after each score.

■ **kiken gachi (martial arts)**
a win because of the opponent's withdrawal during a match. (Judo).

■ **kill (badminton)**
a smash from near the net.

■ **kill (lawn tennis)**
to hit the ball hard into an area where the opponent can't reach it.

■ **kill (table tennis)**
a shot on which the ball is hit as hard as possible, often with topspin. See also loop kill.

■ **kiotsuke (martial arts)**
attention; a command.

■ **kip (gymnastics)**
a move from below the apparatus to above it.

■ **kiritsu (martial arts)**
stand up; a command.

■ **knee touch (weightlifting)**
the act of touching the knee to the platform in the course of a lift, an illegal act that results in no lift.

■ **kneeing (icehockey)**
a minor penalty which occurs when a player uses a knee to hit his opponent in the leg, thigh or lower body.

■ **knife in (rowing)**
see *dig deep*.

■ **knock down (equestrian)**
to hit a fence, gate or any other obstacle, causing it to fall.

■ **knock forward (rugby)**
same as *knock on*.

■ **knock-on (rugby)**
a mishandling of the ball, while attempting to catch a kick or pass, so that it touches the ground in front of the player or knocking the ball forward from another player's hand. The ball is awarded to the opponents in a scrum for an unintentional knock-on. The opponents are given a penalty kick from the spot for an intentional knock-on.

■ **knuckle ball (baseball)**
a pitch thrown by gripping one of the seams on a ball with fingernails and/or knuckles of the forefinger and middle finger with the thumb another fingers underneath the ball. The ball is pushed out of the hand by the two fingers to keep the ball from rotating, causing the ball to move in an unpredictable manner.

■ **knurl (weightlifting)**
the roughened pattern on the barbell's surface that makes gripping it easier and more secure.

■ **ko kutsu dachi (martial arts)**
a defensive stance in which most of the weight is on the back leg.

■ **Kodokan (martial arts)**
the world headquarters of judo, in Japan, a seven-story building that includes a 100 by 100-foot hall with 500 mats.

■ **koka (martial arts)**
a near yuko. However, kokas cannot be accumulated to make a higher score. (Judo).

■ **kumite (martial arts)**
free style sparring.

■ **kumite dashi (martial arts)**
fighting stance.

■ **kung fu (martial arts)**
westerners have given this name to a conglomeration of Chinese fighting styles.

■ **kuzushi (martial arts)**
the act of throwing the opponent off balance.

■ **kyu (martial arts)**
a grade under black belt. First kyu is the highest and 10th is the lowest.

■ **kyusho-jitsu (martial arts)**
techniques for striking pressure points.

■ **lame (fencing)**
a metallic vest/jacket used to detect valid touches in foil and sabre.

■ **lane press (water polo)**
a defense in which players are positioned in passing lanes, between the ball and the players they are guarding, rather than between the offensive players and the goal.

■ **lap (cycling)**
one trip around a track that is traversed more than once during a race.

■ **late cut (cricket)**
a hit that is executed by a batter by deflecting the pitch in a slicing motion, just before it reaches the wicket keeper or catcher.

■ **lateral (football)**
a pass thrown to a teammate backwards from the team's line of scrimmage or parallel to it; unlike a forward pass (which can be thrown only once per play), players may lateral the ball as often as they want.

■ **lath (equestrian)**
a thin white strip that marks the boundary of a water jump. It's lined with plasticine to show whether a horse's hoof touched it.

■ **lawn tennis (lawn tennis)**
the original name for modern tennis, based on the fact that it's played on grass, to distinguish it from court tennis.

■ **layback (rowing)**
the backward lean of an oarsman's body at the end of a stroke.

■ layout (gymnastics)

a position in which the body is extended to full length, either straight or slightly arched.

■ layup or layin (basketball)

a shot taken after driving to the basket by leaping up under the basket and using one hand to drop the ball directly into the basket (layin) or to bank the ball off the backboard into it (layup).

■ lbw (leg before wicket) (cricket)

a pitch which is intercepted by a batter's body before it hits the sticks an umpire will rule the batter out if he is sure that the sticks would have been hit.

■ lead (equestrian)

the leg that leads during the canter. The inside foreleg reaches the farthest during a correct lead.

■ lead change (equestrian)

a maneuver in which the horse's lead foot changes.

■ lead out (cycling)

to sprint in front of another rider, almost always a teammate, so that rider can take advantage of the draft for a time, before coming past with an even faster sprint toward the finish.

■ lead pass (icehockey)

a pass sent ahead of a moving teammate designed to meet the player at the location he is headed.

■ leading the receiver (basketball)

when a passer throws the ball where he thinks a receiver is headed.

■ league (rugby)

a version of rugby with 13 players and different rules

than are used in rugby union.

■ left court (lawn tennis)
same as *advantage court.*

■ left on base (baseball)
runners stranded on base after three outs.

■ leg break (cricket)
a pitch that is thrown almost like baseball's screwballand breaks into a batter's body off the bounce, from the batter's leg side.

■ leg bye (cricket)
run (s) scored when the ball hits the batter's legs and goes off into the field . The runs are added to the team total as extras, but not credited to batters. nor charged to bowlers. Leg-byes are not allowed when there is an lbw

out or if the ball has been intentionally kicked or deflected by the batter.

■ leg glance (cricket)
a hit consisiting of a deflection around the batter's legs, of a pitch past the wicket keeper (catcher) and behind him.

■ leg shot (wrestling)
a quick move, involving a level change, in which a wrestler thrusts toward the opponent's legs in an attempt to get a lock on one or both of them.

■ leg side (cricket)
that half of the field, as bisected by a line joining the wickets and extended both ways, where the batter's legs are placed. Also called on side.

■ leg up (rugby)
descriptive of an offense in which the hooker puts his foot into the tunnel of a scrum before the scrumhalf feeds the ball.

■ **let (badminton)**
an official stoppage in play after which a rally is replayed.

■ **let (lawn tennis)**
a stroke that doesn't count and must be replayed. This most commonly happens when a serve touches the net before entering the proper service court. It's also a let if the serve is delivered before the receiver is ready, if play is interrupted by some unusual occurrence (such as an animal running onto the court)or if a linesman's decision that resulted in stoppage of play is reversed by the umpire.

■ **let (table tennis)**
a rally whose result doesn't count, usually because the umpire called a halt in play because of some distraction or interruption.

■ **let it run! (rowing)**
a call from the coxswain to stop rowing at the finish, letting the boat glide through the water and coast to a stop.

■ **let serve (table tennis)**
a serve that touches the net before entering the opponent's court. It doesn't count and is replayed.

■ **level change (wrestling)**
bending at the knees to raise or lower the hips in order to get into a new position for a hold or takedown move.

■ **lie (icehockey)**
angle made by the shaft of the stick and the blade.

■ **lift (wrestling)**
to take an opponent entirely off the mat.

■ **lightweight (rowing)**
a weight division for lighter rowers. In the Olympics, 72.5 kilograms (about 160 pounds) or less for men and 59 kilograms (about 130 pounds) or less for women.

■ **limited and unlimited over games (cricket)**
limited over games are those where each team is allowed to bat only for a designated number of overs. Typically, 30, 40, 45 or 50 overs are set

as the limit for each team's innings. Unlimited over games are those where no over restriction is placed on a team's innings.

■ line (fencing)
the main direction of an attack (eg., high/low, inside/outside), often equated to the parry that must be made to deflect the attack; also point in line.

■ line change (icehockey)
the entire forward line and/or defensive line will be replaced at once, which puts players on the ice who work well together.

■ line drive (baseball)
a ball hit in the air at a low projectory directly to a fielder or through the infield.

■ line judge (lawn tennis)
an official who is responsible for determining whether or not a shot landed in the court. They include the baseline judges, service line judges and sideline judges.

■ line of scrimmage (football)
an imaginary line which no player may cross before the snap; each team has its own line of scrimmage, separated by the neutral zone.

■ lineman (football)
a player who starts each play within 1 yard of his line of scrimmage.

■ lineout (rugby)
the method of putting the ball back into play after it has gone out of bounds. The two sets of forwards line up opposite each other; a player from one side then calls a play and throws the ball between the two lines.

■ linesmen (icehockey)
the two officials on the ice, one toward each end of the rink, responsible for infractions of the rules concerning off-side plays at the blue lines or centre line and for any icing violations; they conduct most of the face-offs, sometimes advise the referee concerning penalties and sepa-

rate players who are fighting; they wear black pants and an official league sweater and are on skates.

■ **line-up (baseball)**
a team's batting order and fielding positions.

■ **link (field hockey)**
a midfielder.

■ **live ball (basketball)**
as soon as a ball is given to a free-throw shooter or a thrower on a throw-in, it is live, but the game clock does not restart until the ball is alive.

■ **live ball (football)**
a ball becomes live as soon as it is snapped or free kicked (as in a kickoff); opposite of a dead ball.

■ **live time (water polo)**
a period when the clock is running. Compare dead time.

■ **liverpool (equestrian)**
a water jump that has a pole over it or just beyond it.

■ **loaded (table tennis)**
descriptive of a shot that has a great deal of spin.

■ **lob (lawn tennis)**
a shot that is hit in a high arc, usually over the opponent's head. See *defensive lob; offensive lob.*

■ **lob (table tennis)**
a shot that's hit high into the air, often as a way of buying time after the opponent has hit a kill shot.

■ **lock (rugby)**
one of two forwards, who usually wear Nos. 4 and 5and generally the two largest players on a team.

■ **lofted drive (cricket)**
a drive where the ball is lofted (hit in the air) to clear infield or midfield positions.

■ **long (lawn tennis)**
descriptive of a shot that is out because it hits the court beyond the opponent's baseline.

■ **long corner (field hockey)**
if a defending player unintentionally kicks the ball over

the back line, it is put in play on the back line about 5 metres from the corner flag and the attacking team is given possession.

■ **long hop or short pitch (cricket)**
a pitch that is bounced far away from the batter (at least 7 to 10 yards away), so it reaches the batter after a long hopor bounce.

■ **long pips rubber (table tennis)**
a rubber sheet covered with long, cylindrical projections (pips) that allow the player to put a lot of unpredictable spin on the ball.

■ **loom (rowing)**
the section of the oar between the blade and the handle.

■ **loop (table tennis)**
a shot hit with a long, upward motion, from as low as the knees to as high as the forehead, grazing the ball and putting heavy topspin on it. It's often used to set up a kill, since the opponent's return is likely to be high.

■ **loop kill (table tennis)**
a loop hit very hard, with a flat trajectory.

■ **loose ball (basketball)**
a ball that is alive but not in the possession of either team.

■ **loose ball (football)**
a ball that is not in possession of either team, such as after a fumble or a kickoff; it can be recovered by either team.

■ **loose forwards (rugby)**
the flankers and the No. 8 forward.

■ **loosehead (rugby)**
the No. 1 prop in a scrum.

■ **lot number (weightlifting)**
the number assigned to a competitor during the draw.

■ **love (lawn tennis)**
zero; no points. For example, a score of 40-love means that the server has scored three points and the receiver hasn't scored any. In a set score, it

means that the player hasn't won any games. Probably derived from the old French word for egg, l'ove, because a zero is egg-shaped.

love game (lawn tennis)
a game in which the loser scored no points.

love set (lawn tennis)
a set in which the loser won no games.

low post (basketball)
an imaginary area outside either side of the foul lane close to the basket.

lower percentage shot (basketball)
a shot that is less likely to go in the basket, such as one thrown by a player who is off balance or outside his shooting range.

lunge (fencing)
an attack made by extending the rear legand landing on the bent front leg.

lunge (rowing)
an abrupt lean of the body before the catch, which can throw the oarsmen out of timing with the rest of the crew.

madison (cycling)
a track race of a specific duration in time, ranging from six hours to six days, for teams of two or three riders. The winner is the team covering the greatest distance in the specified time. Only one rider from each team is on the track at any given time. A rider goes as fast as possible for one or two laps, then leaves the track and is replaced by another member of the team. A unique feature of the Madison is that the rider who leaves the track hurls the teammate into the race by using a special handle in the rear pocket of the teammate's racing shorts. The event is named for Madison Square Garden, where six-day bicycle races originated.

maiden over (cricket)
a set of six pitches delivered by a bowler in which no earned runs are scored.

■ major penalty (icehockey)
a type of individual penalty called for more serious infractions of the rules; of 5 minutes in duration whether or not the non-penalised team scores.

■ maloney (gymnastics)
a piked circle through a handst and with a flight from the low bar to a hang on the high bar. Named for U. S. gymnast Kristen Maloney, who created it.

■ mal-parry (fencing)
also mal-pare'; a parry that fails to prevent the attack from landing.

■ man-down (water polo)
descriptive of the 20-second period when the defensive team is one player short because of an exclusion foul.

■ man-in-motion (football)
a single player on the offense who is permitted to move prior to the snap; he may only run parallel to the line of scrimmage or away from it.

■ manipulators (fencing)
the thumb and index finger of the sword hand.

■ man-to-man defense (basketball)
the defensive style where each defensive player is responsible for guarding one opponent.

■ man-up (water polo)
descriptive of the 20-second period when the offensive team has one player more than the defensive team because of an exclusion foul.

■ maraging (fencing)
a special steel used for making blades; said to be stronger and break more cleanly than conventional steels.

■ march madness (basketball)
see *NCAA Tournament.*

■ **mark (field hockey)**
to guard an opponent closely.

■ **mark (rugby)**
the spot designated by the referee as the location for a scrum.

■ **marker points (fencing)**
an old method of detecting hits using inked points.

■ **martingale (fencing)**
a strap that binds the grip to the wrist/forearm.

■ **mass start (cycling)**
descriptive of a race in which all the riders start at the same time. Among the types of races that have mass starts are the scratch race, the points raceand the miss-and-out.

■ **master of ceremonies (weightlifting)**
see *speaker*.

■ **mat (wrestling)**
the mat for international wrestling competition has a central wrestling area, 9 meters in diameter, with a centre circle 1 metre in diameter. Inside the contest area is a red band, 1 metre wide, known as the passivity zone.

■ **matae (martial arts)**
stop; a command.

■ **match (fencing)**
the aggregate of bouts between two fencing teams.

■ **match (lawn tennis)**
a tennis contest made up of sets, as a set is made up of games. In major competition, a men's match is made up of five sets and the winner is the player who first wins three sets. Women usually play best-of-three matches.

■ **match (rugby)**
a match is made up of two halves, each 40 minutes long, plus injury time. Teams change ends after a five-minute break.

■ **match (table tennis)**
a series of games played to determine a winner, typically best-of-three or best-of-five.

■ match (wrestling)

1) A series of matches between two teams, involving wrestlers from different weight classes. 2) A bout.

■ match point (lawn tennis)

a point that will end the match if it is won by the leading player or side. See also *set point; game point.*

■ match sprint (cycling)

a race, usually of 1 kilometre, in which two riders compete against one another. The match sprint is conducted like a tournament, with the winners of one round of heats advancing to the next round until only two remain to compete for the championship. However, riders who lose in the first heat are often given a second chance, called the repechage.

■ match-up (icehockey)

a pairing of players on opposing teams who will cover each other during the hockey game.

■ match-ups (basketball)

any pairing of players on opposing teams who guard each other.

■ maul (rugby)

when a runner has come into contact with opponents and cannot advance the ball further, players may bind themselves into a maul. There must be at least three players bound. The maul ends when the ball is on the ground; when the ball or the player who had been carrying it emerges from the maul; or when a scrum is ordered. A maul is similar to a ruck, except that the ball is not on the ground.

■ measure (fencing)

the distance between the fencers.

■ meet (wrestling)

an organised competition involving wrestlers from two or more teams.

■ men's doubles (table tennis)

doubles competition between male teams.

■ midcourt (badminton)
the middle third of the court.

■ midcourt (lawn tennis)
the area of the court in the vicinity of the service line.

■ middle (fencing)
the middle third of the blade, between foible and forte.

■ midfield (football)
the 50-yard line, which divides the length of the field in half.

■ midfielder (field hockey)
a player who plays both offense and defense, patrolling the middle area of the field. Also known as a halfback.

■ miller (gymnastics)
a maneuver on the balance beam, a back dive with a quarter twist to a handstand, followed by a half pirouette. Named for U. S. gymnast Shannon Miller, who created it.

■ mini-break (lawn tennis)
loss of a point on service during a tie-breaker.

■ minor penalty (icehockey)
a type of penalty lasting 2 minutes; if the non-penalised team scores a power play goal during this time, the penalty ends immediately.

■ misbehaviour (table tennis)
this includes unsportsmanlike conduct such as using abusive language, deliberately breaking the ball, kicking the tableand showing disrespect toward the officials. The first offense generally brings a yellow card, the second a penalty point for the player's opponent, the third two penalty points. Any misbehaviour beyond the third offense is likely to result in suspension.

■ misconduct (field hockey)
offenses that include intentional violations, time-wasting, rough or dangerous play or any bad behaviour. Green, yellow or red cards may be issued for misconduct.

■ miss water (rowing)
to have too short a drive, usually caused by not getting the blade into the water quickly enough at the catch.

■ miss-and-out (cycling)
a type of mass start race in which the last rider across the finish line after each lap or circuit is eliminated. When a predetermined number of riders remain, they take part in a sprint to determine the winner.

■ mixed doubles (lawn tennis)
doubles competition in which each team is made up of one female and one male player.

■ mixed doubles (table tennis)
doubles competition in which each team has a male and a female player.

■ morote gari (martial arts)
a throw in which the attacker wraps his arms around the opponent's legs and pushes his shoulder into the opponent's abdomen to take him down backwards.

■ motorpace (cycling)
a popular type of race in Europe, in which each rider is behind a small motorcycle or moped, which provides a slipstream.

■ moulinet (fencing)
a whirling cut, executed from the wrist or elbow.

■ mound (baseball)
hill the pitcher stands on while pitching.

■ movement (equestrian)
any single characteristic style of a horse's motion. A number of such movements go into a dressage performance.

■ moving pick (water polo)
a move in which an offensive player swims in front of a player defending another offensive player, freeing that teammate to receive a pass or take a shot.

■ MVP (Most Valuable Player) (basketball)
an award recognising the NBA player who contributed

most to the regular season or to the Finals.

■ **nage waza (martial arts)**
defensive throwing techniques that make use of the attacker's momentum. Mainly judo.

■ **nail (gymnastics)**
same as stick.

■ **national hockey league (NHL) (icehockey)**
a professional league started on November 22, 1917; currently contains 30 teams in the U.S. and Canada.

■ **natural aids (equestrian)**
subtle body signals given to the horse by the rider's seat, hands and legs, as well as voice commands.

■ **natural goal (water polo)**
a goal scored from open play with both teams at full strength. Excludes goals made on penalty shots or when a team is a man up.

■ **NBA (National Basketball Association) (basketball)**
a professional league created in 1949 that now has 27 teams in the U.S. and is adding 2 Canadian teams in 1995.

■ **NCAA (National Collegiate Athletic Association) (basketball)**
a voluntary association of over 1,200 colleges and universities in the U.S. whose role is to establish standards and protect the integrity of amateurism for student-athletes.

■ **NCAA Tournament (basketball)**
an annual competition between 64 college teams to crown a national champion; also called March Madness because the three-week-long event is held during March; see also Final Four.

■ **near fall (wrestling)**
if a wrestler exposes the opponent's shoulders four inches or less above the mat or has one of the opponent's shoulders on the mat and the

other at an angle of less than 45 degrees to the mat, it is a near fall, worth two technical points.

■ necessary line (football)
the imaginary line the offense must cross to achieve a new first down.

■ net (icehockey)
the goal; netting attached to the goalposts and frame of the goal to trap the puck when a goal is scored.

■ net (lawn tennis)
the barrier that divides a tennis court into lengthwise halves. It's a web, usually made of braided synthetic material, suspended from a steel cable that's strung between two 3½-foot metal posts located 3 feet outside the sidelines. The cable is covered by a band of canvas or synthetic material, 2 to 2 1/2 inches wide. A 2-inch wide centre strap, also made of canvas or synthetic material, holds the net taut at the centre. As a verb, to net means to hit the ball into the net.

■ net (table tennis)
the net is 6 inches high and stretches the width of the table.

■ net cord (lawn tennis)
the cable that supports the net.

■ net cord judge (lawn tennis)
an official who is responsible for calling lets on service. This judge sits in front of the umpire's chair, at one end of the net and rests one hand on top of the net in order to feel vibrations set up if the ball hits the net cord. Also called net judge.

■ net game (lawn tennis)
a playing style in which the player takes every opportunity to rush the net. To be contrasted with baseline game.

■ **net man (lawn tennis)**
in doubles, the partner who is stationed near the net during his or her partner's service.

■ **neutral position (wrestling)**
the position wrestlers take at the beginning of a match, standing and facing each other, but not in contact. Also known as standing position.

■ **neutral support (cycling)**
assistance that is given to a rider by someone other than a teammate. In road races and time trials, a follow truck carries a mechanic, spare tires and other parts in order to offer neutral support to riders who have mechanical problems. In mountain bike racing, however, neutral support is against the rules and results in disqualification.

■ **neutral throw (water polo)**
a throw by a referee that gives each team an equal chance to reach the ball. A neutral throw is most often used after a double foul.

■ **neutral zone (icehockey)**
the area between the blue lines.

■ **neutral zone (football)**
the region that contains the ball as it sits on the ground before each play; the area between the two lines of scrimmage.

■ **neuvieme (fencing)**
an unconventional parry sometimes described as blade behind the back, pointing down (a variant of octave), other times similar to elevated sixte.

■ **NFL (National Football League) (football)**
the major professional football league in the U.S. with 32 teams; its headquarters are in New York.

■ **NFL Championship (football)**
the game held from 1933 through 1965 to decide the champion of professional football; renamed the Super Bowl in 1966.

■ nickel defense (football)
when a defense brings in a 5th defensive back to replace a linebacker on the field, increasing its pass coverage.

■ night watchman (cricket)
in matches/games lasting 2 or more days, a lower order batter, who is sent in to stall for time late in the evening, so the more experienced batters can bat the following day.

■ NIT (National Invitational Tournament) (basketball)
the oldest college tournament, in which 32 teams not selected to the NCAA Tournament compete each year.

■ no hitter (baseball)
a game in which a pitcher does not allow the opposing team to reach a base via a safe hit.

■ no lift (weightlifting)
an attempt judged invalid by at least two of the three referees.

■ no-ball (cricket)
a pitch delivered by a pitcher who has crossed the line he is supposed to pitch fromor violated some other rule. When an umpire calls no ball, the batter cannot be out except when running and gets tagged.

■ no-man's land (lawn tennis)
the area between the baseline and the service line, so called because a player who is caught there finds it difficult to hit ground strokes and isn't close enough to the net to hit slams.

■ noodle (cycling)
to ride at a relatively slow, easy pace.

■ norris division (icehockey)
with the Smythe Division made up the Campbell Con-

ference until the 1992-93 season; renamed the Central Division of the Western Conference starting with the 1993-94 season.

■ **not up (lawn tennis)**
said of a ball that is hit just as it's bouncing for the second time. Results in loss of point.

■ **number 8 (rugby)**
the forward who wears that number binds into the scrum, usually between the two locks and is responsible for initiating attacks by the forwards or for getting the ball to the scrumhalf.

■ **o goshi (martial arts)**
a basic hip throw.

■ **o guruma (martial arts)**
a wheel throw, on which the opponent is slung vertically around the attacker's waist.

■ **oar (rowing)**
a pole with a flat section, known as the blade, near the end, used for propelling a boat through the water.

■ **oarlock (rowing)**
a latch that holds the oar and provides a fulcrum for the stroke.

■ **oarsman (rowing)**
a rower of either sex.

■ **obi (martial arts)**
the sash that holds the jacket closed. (Judo).

■ **obi goshi (martial arts)**
throwing the opponent by grasping his belt or sash.

■ **obstacle (equestrian)**
any object that a horse must clear to complete the course in show jumping and the three-day event, such as a fence, gate or water jump.

■ **obstruction (field hockey)**
field hockey players may not use their sticks or bodies to prevent other players from hitting the ball. Doing so is obstruction. It's also obstruction if the goalkeeper lies on the ball. See also third-party obstruction.

■ **obstruction (rugby)**
getting in the way of an opponent who's chasing the ball. Also called blocking.

■ **obstruction (table tennis)**
touching the ball with any part of the body or clothing while it is over the table and before it has bounced in the proper court. The offender loses the point.

■ **octave (fencing)**
blade down and to the outside, wrist supinated.

■ **odi (cricket)**
a one-day International, an official limited-over cricket game (typically 50 overs per team) where the contenders are accredited national teams.

■ **off drive (cricket)**
a drive which is executed at about a 45-degree angle to the line of the wickets, on the batter's off side.

■ **off keel (rowing)**
descriptive of an unbalanced boat.

■ **off side (cricket)**
that half of the field, as bisected by a line joining the wickets and extended both ways, which is in front of and away from the batter, i.e. the other half of the field (as opposed to his leg or on side).

■ **off the dribble (basketball)**
a shot taken while driving to the basket.

■ **off-break (cricket)**
a pitch which, after bouncing, breaks into the batter's body from his off side (see definition below for off side).

■ **offending team (football)**
the team that committed a foul.

■ **offense (basketball)**
the team with possession of the ball.

■ **offensive lob (lawn tennis)**
a lob that is an attempt to score, rather than being purely defensive. It's typically hit very deep into the

opponent's court when the opponent is at the net.

■ **offensive rebound (basketball)**
a rebound of a team's own missed shot.

■ **offensive volley (lawn tennis)**
a volley, usually hit from above the netthat's meant to score a point.

■ **official (rowing)**
an administrator who follows the race in a motorboat

to ensure that all boats stay in their designated lanes.

■ **officials (basketball)**
the crew chief, referee and umpire who control the game, stop and start play and impose penalties for violations and fouls.

■ **officials (icehockey)**
two referees and two linesmen on the ice calling infractions and handing out penalties plus several off-ice officials including two goal judges, the game timekeeper, the penalty timekeeper, the official scorer, the statistician and the video goal judge.

■ **offside (icehockey)**
a violation which occurs when both skates of an attacking player cross the opponent's blue line before the puck is passed or carried into the attacking zone; also called when a player passes the puck from his defending zone to a teammate across the red centre line (two-line pass); this is one of the most common calls made in a hockey game and results in a face-off.

■ **offside (rugby)**
a violation committed when a player crosses the gain line during a lineout, maul, ruck or scrum before it has been completed or when a player is in front of the ball while it

is played by a teammate. A penalty is called if an offside player then plays the ball, obstructs or tackles an opponentor is within 10 meters of an opponent waiting for the ball. The other side is awarded a penalty kick from the spot of infringement or a scrum at the place where the offending side last played the ball.

■ **offside pass (icehockey)**
see *two-line pass*.

■ **offside (football)**
when any part of a player's body is beyond his line of scrimmage when the ball is snapped; a foul punishable by a 5-yard penalty.

■ **Olympic sprint (cycling)**
a pursuit race between teams of three riders each. After one lap, the lead rider leaves the track. After the second lap, another rider leaves and the last rider continues for a third lap to the finish line.

■ **on deck (baseball)**
a term used to refer to the next batter up in the inning. This person stands in a designated circular area and warms up before batting.

■ **on downs (football)**
the term used to describe a team's loss of possession if it fails to reach the necessary line on a fourth down play.

■ **on drive (cricket)**
a drive which is executed at about a 45-degree angle to the line of the wickets, on the batter's on or leg side.

■ **on keel (rowing)**
descriptive of a balanced and level boat.

■ **on the bit (equestrian)**
descriptive of a horse that's being restrained by pressure on the bit.

■ **on the flat (equestrian)**
descriptive of training or rounding over ground without obstacles.

■ **on the road (icehockey)**
when an NHL team plays games away from its home arena.

■ **on-the-fly (icehockey)**
making player changes or substitutions while play is under way.

■ **open (basketball)**
when a player is unguarded by a defender.

■ **open (wrestling)**
a command from the referee telling a wrestler to change his position and adopt more open tactics. If the wrestler doesn't respond, the referee will issue a caution for passive obstruction.

■ **open grip (lawn tennis)**
a grip in which the racket face is tilted upward, away from the court.

■ **open ice (icehockey)**
that part of the ice that is free of opponents.

■ **open paddle (table tennis)**
a paddle tilted upward, away from the table. Striking the ball with an open paddle tends to produce backspin.

■ **open racket (lawn tennis)**
a racket held with an open grip.

■ **open receiver (football)**
a player who has no defender closely covering him.

■ **open tournament (lawn tennis)**
in the early days of tennis, clubs held two types of tournaments: Closed, to which only club members were admitted and open, which nonmembers could also enter. With the advent of professionalism, open came to mean a tournament that could be entered by amateurs and professionals alike. Today, all major tournaments are opens.

■ **opening batsman (cricket)**
one of the first two batters sent in to start a team's innings.

■ **opposition (fencing)**
holding the opponent's blade in a non-threatening line; a time-hit; any attack or

counter-attack with opposition.

■ **optionals (gymnastics)**
routines designed by the gymnast.

■ **ordinary foul (water polo)**
an infringement that usually results in a free throw for the opposing team. Ordinary fouls include taking the ball underwater when tackled; playing the ball while standing or walking on the bottom of the pool; jumping from the bottom of the pool; hitting the ball with the fist; playing the ball with both hands at the same time; and deliberately impeding an opponent who doesn't have the ball.

■ **osae komi waza (martial arts)**
techniques of immobilising and pinning the opponent.

■ **out (lawn tennis)**
descriptive of a shot that lands outside the playing area, wide and/or long.

■ **out half (rugby)**
same as *fly half*.

■ **out in order (baseball)**
retiring the first 3 batters in an inning.

■ **out of bounds (basketball)**
the area outside of and including the end lines and sidelines.

■ **out of bounds (rugby)**
the ball is out of bounds when it crosses a touch-line or a dead-ball line.

■ **out of bounds (football)**
the region of the field touching or outside the sidelines and end lines; as soon as a ball carrier or the ball itself touches out of bounds, the play is over.

■ outboard (rowing)
the distance from the oarlock to the tip of the oar's blade.

■ outfield (baseball)
area between the back edge of the infield and home run fence.

■ outfielder (baseball)
a fielder who occupies a position in the outfield, which is the playing field most distance from home base.

■ outlet (water polo)
a pass from the goalkeeper to a teammate to begin a counterattack after a save.

■ outrigger (rowing)
see *rigger*.

■ outside centre (rugby)
the back who usually wears No. 13. *See centre.*

■ outside half (rugby)
same as *fly half*.

■ outside hand (rowing)
the hand farthest from the oarlock.

■ outside shooting (basketball)
shots taken from the perimeter.

■ outswing (cricket)
a pitch which moves down and away from the batter in the air, like baseball's slider.

■ over (cricket)
the set of six pitches delivered from one wicket to the other by a pitcher.

■ over the limit (basketball)
when a team commits 5 or more team fouls per NBA period (4 in each overtime); 8 or more per WNBA half; 7 or more per half in college; this team is also said to be in the penalty.

■ overhand grip (weightlifting)
a grip in which the palms face backwards.

■ overhead (lawn tennis)
a shot hit much like a serve, when the ball is above the player's head, usually a smash. It's often used by a player at net or in the forecourt against a lob that hasn't been hit deep enough.

■ **overpitch (cricket)**

a pitch which is pitched so far forward that the batter can reach the point where it bounced by a forward step.

■ **overspin (lawn tennis)**

topspin.

■ **overtime (field hockey)**

if a game ends in a tie, teams may play a sudden-death, ten-minute overtime period, with the victory going to the first team that scores a goal.

■ **overtime (icehockey)**

an additional period of play used to break a tie.

■ **overtime loss (icehockey)**

the result for a team that loses a game in overtime that was tied after regulation; this category was created starting with the 1999-2000 season and is worth 1 point in the standings.

■ **overtime or OT (basketball)**

the extra period (s) played after a regulation game ends tied.

■ **overtime period (wrestling)**

if the score is tied or neither wrestler has three points when time runs out on a bout, a three-minute overtime period begins immediately. The first wrestler to score a point wins.

■ **oxer (equestrian)**

a fence with two or more vertical jumps several feet apart.

■ **pace (lawn tennis)**

the speed at which the ball is hit. It's commonly used to mean a great deal of speed, but in fact a well-paced shot may be hit rather slowly. A common tactic against a hard-hitting opponent is to vary the pace from one shot to the next.

■ **pace line (cycling)**

a group of riders, usually in an echelon, who take turns setting the pace so that the others can draft on the leader.

■ pack (rugby)
the eight forwards when they are bound for a scrum. It consists of three front row players, two second row players and three back row players.

■ paddle (rowing)
to row gently, with minimum force.

■ paddle (table tennis)
the table tennis paddle must be made primarily of wood. There are no restrictions as to size. A legal rubber sheet must be applied to any side used for striking the ball. One side must be black, the other cherry red. If there is a non-hitting side with no rubber sheet attached, it must have a paint sheet of the appropriate colour.

■ paint sheet (table tennis)
not paint at all, but a sheet of coloured plastic used to cover the non-hitting side of the paddle.

■ pair (lawn tennis)
a doubles team.

■ pair (rowing)
a sweep-oar boat for two rowers. There is competition for pairs with coxswain and pairs without coxswain.

■ pak salto (gymnastics)
a high bar move in which the gymnast releases the bar, does a backward flip and catches the low bar. Named for North Korean gymnast Gyong Sil Pak, who created it.

■ par terre (wrestling)
a re-starting position in which a wrestler is on the mat, on hands and knees and the other wrestler kneels beside him, with both hands on his back. (French for on the ground.).

■ parallel bars (gymnastics)
1) A piece of apparatus consisting of two bars, each 195 centimetres high and 350 centimetres long and positioned 42 to 52 centimetres apart. 2) A men's event performed on the apparatus. A routine is made up mostly of swing and flight elements,

including at least one release move, which includes a release and a re-grasp.

■ parallel oxer (equestrian)

an obstacle that has front and back rails of equal height, set wide apart to produce a spread.

■ parry (fencing)

a block of the attack, made with the forte of one's own blade; also parade.

■ partner (lawn tennis)

one of the two players on a doubles team.

■ partnership stand (cricket)

used to indicate the number of runs scored by both batters on base, between one out and the next one. for example, a partnership of 100 runs for the third wicket would mean that 100 runs were scored by both batters between the second and third out.

■ pass (basketball)

when a passer throws the ball to a teammate; used to start plays, move the ball downcourt, keep it away from defenders and get it to a shooter.

■ pass (fencing)

an attack made with a cross; eg. fleche. Also, the act of moving past the opponent.

■ pass (lawn tennis)

to hit a shot that goes past the opponent, usually when the opponent is at or near the net.

■ pass back (field hockey)

the centre pass.

■ pass defender (football)

a defensive player who covers an opposing receiver.

■ pass patterns or pass

routes (football)
pre-determined paths receivers follow to help the passer quickly locate them so he can more easily get them the ball.

■ **pass protection (football)**
blocking by offensive players to keep defenders away from the quarterback on passing plays.

■ **pass rush (football)**
a surge by defenders to get past blockers and sack the quarterback.

■ **passage (equestrian)**
a slow motion, suspended trot in which the pairs of feet diagonally opposite one another are raised and returned to the ground in alternation.

■ **passata-sotto (fencing)**
a lunge made by dropping one hand to the floor.

■ **passe' (fencing)**
an attack that passes the target without hitting; also a cross-step (see cross).

■ **passed ball (baseball)**
a pitched ball missed by the catcher, allowing a runner to advance.

■ **passer (basketball)**
the player who passes the ball to a teammate.

■ **passing (icehockey)**
when one player uses his stick to send the puck to a teammate.

■ **passing shot (lawn tennis)**
a shot that passes the opponent.

■ **passive obstruction (wrestling)**
if a wrestler continually obstructs the opponent's holds, holds both the opponent's hands, continually lies flat on the mator deliberately runs off the mat, it is passive obstruction. The opponent is given three choices: 1) To place the offender in the bottom position in par terre; 2) To continue the bout from the neutral position; 3) To assume the down positon in par terre.

■ **passivity (wrestling)**
another name for passive obstruction.

■ **passivity zone (wrestling)**
the outer band, 1 metre wide, outside the central wrestling area.

■ **passout (icehockey)**
a pass by an attacking player from behind his opponent's net or goal line to a teammate in front of the net.

■ **patrick division (icehockey)**
with the Adams Division made up the Wales Conference until the 1992-93 season; renamed the Atlantic Division of the Eastern Conference starting with the 1993-94 season.

■ **peloton (cycling)**
the field.

■ **penalty (icehockey)**
punishment of a player for a violation of the rules, resulting in suspension from the game for a period of time; 6 types exist (icehockey) minor, bench, major, misconduct, match and goalkeeper's penalties.

■ **penalty box (icehockey)**
an area with a bench just off the ice, behind the sideboards outside the playing area where penalised players serve their penalty time.

■ **penalty corner (field hockey)**
when a defending player deliberately hits the ball over the back line, the attacking team is awarded a penalty corner. The ball is placed on the goal line at least 10 yards from the goal and an offensive player is given a free hit from that point.

■ **penalty foul (water polo)**
a foul that results in a penalty throw for the opposing team. Penalty fouls include: A foul committed by a defending player behind the four-meter line that is judged to have prevented a goal from being scored; an act of brutality behind the four-meter line; or pulling the

goal over with the object of preventing a score.

■ penalty kick (rugby)
an uncontested kick awarded for a major infraction. It can be taken directly on goal and is worth 3 points if successful.

■ penalty killer (icehockey)
a player expert at backchecking and keeping or gaining control of a loose puck under difficult circumstances who is trained to break up a power play when his team is shorthanded.

■ penalty point (equestrian)
see *fault*.

■ penalty point (lawn tennis)
see *point penalty*.

■ penalty point (table tennis)
a point awarded by the umpire to a player because of a rules violation by that player's opponent. A penalty point can be awarded for a second misbehaviour offense, after the player has been cautioned with a yellow card for the first offense. A third offense incurs two penalty points.

■ penalty points (wrestling)
points used in a negative scoring system, under which the wrestler with the fewest points wins. They're essentially the same as technical points, but they go to the other wrestler. For example, the wrestler who suffers a near fall is given two penalty points.

■ penalty shootout (water polo)
if a game is tied after two overtime periods, a penalty shootout determines the result. Each team gets five penalty throws, which are taken in alternation. Each penalty throw is taken by a different team member. If the score remains tied after the round of penalty throws, the teams alternate shots until one team scores and the other misses.

■ **penalty shot (icehockey)**
a free shot awarded a player who was illegally interfered with, preventing him from a clear scoring opportunity; the shot is taken with only the goalie guarding against it.

■ **penalty shot (water polo)**
see *penalty throw.*

■ **penalty stroke (field hockey)**
if a defending player fouls an opponent in the goal circle, a penalty stroke is awarded. The ball is placed 7 yards (6.4 meters) from the goal and only the goalkeeper is allowed to defend.

■ **penalty throw (water polo)**
a throw taken from the four-metre line by a member of the attacking team, with the goalkeeper as the only defender.

■ **penalty try (rugby)**
a try that is awarded because the opposing side committed a flagrant violation to prevent an obvious try from being scored.

■ **penholder grip (table tennis)**
a grip, especially popular in Asia, in which the racket is held between the thumb and first finger, with the handle pointing up.

■ **perfect game (baseball)**
a game in which a pitcher does not allow any batter of the opposing team to reach base.

■ **perimeter (basketball)**
the area beyond the foul circle away from the basket, including 3-point line, from which players take long-range shots.

■ **period (basketball)**
any quarter, half or overtime segment.

■ **periods (icehockey)**
three 20-minute playing intervals separated by two intermissions.

■ **personal foul (basketball)**
contact between players that may result in injury or provide one team with an unfair

advantage; players may not push, hold, trip, hack, elbow, restrain or charge into an opponent; these are also counted as team fouls.

■ **personal foul (water polo)**
an exclusion foul or penalty foul. If a player commits three personal fouls, he or she is permanently excluded from the game.

■ **personal foul (football)**
a foul that might cause injury; punishable by a 15-yard penalty.

■ **phrase (fencing)**
a set of related actions and reactions in a fencing conversation.

■ **piaffe (equestrian)**
a majestic trot in place, in which the pairs of feet diagonally opposite one another are alternately raised and returned to the ground, while the horse's head is vertical, the neck raised and arched.

■ **pick (table tennis)**
a shot used to turn the opponent's backspin into topspin, effected by using a hitting motion parallel to the table top with an open paddle.

■ **pick off (baseball)**
an attempt by the pitcher to get a base runner out by throwing to the base from the stretch position.

■ **picked off (basketball)**
refers to a defender who has been successfully prevented from reaching the ball handler by an offensive screen.

■ **picked off (football)**
intercepted.

■ **pick-up games (basketball)**
impromptu games played among players who just met.

■ **pickup shot (lawn tennis)**
another name for a half volley.

■ **pike (gymnastics)**
a position in which the body is bent forward at the hips by

more than 90 degrees, while the legs are kept straight.

■ **pin (rowing)**
a metal rod upon which the oarlock is mounted.

■ **pin (wrestling)**
forcing both of the opponent's shoulders to the mat. The result is a fall, which wins the match.

■ **pinch flat (cycling)**
a flat tire caused by hitting an obstacle very hard, so that the inner tube is pinched against the rim.

■ **pinch hitter (baseball)**
a hitter who substitutes in the line-up for a starting player. The original batter can't return to the game, so the pinch hitter or a third person takes over the defensive position as well.

■ **pinch runner (baseball)**
a player entering the game to run for someone already on base.

■ **pineapple tip (fencing)**
a serrated epee point used prior to electric judging.

■ **ping-pong (table tennis)**
a trademarked name for table tennis originally registered by Parker Brothers in 1901.

■ **pips (table tennis)**
small cylinders that protrude from a rubber sheet.

■ **pips out (table tennis)**
descriptive of a rubber sheet attached to the paddle so that the side with pips will contact the ball, as on a hardbat. The opposite of inverted rubber.

■ **pirouette (equestrian)**
a full turn on the spot, with the inside hind foot is the pivot.

■ **pirouette (gymnastics)**
to change direction with a twist in the handstand position. Also used as a noun.

■ **piste (fencing)**
the linear strip on which a fencing bout is fought; approx. 2m wide and 14m long.

■ **pistol grip (fencing)**
a modern or thopaedic grip, shaped vaguely like a small pistol; varieties are known by names such as Belgian, German, Russian and Visconti.

■ **pitch (field hockey)**
the field hockey playing area. The pitch is 100 yards long by 60 yards wide, divided by a centre line and two 25-yard lines, one in each half of the field.

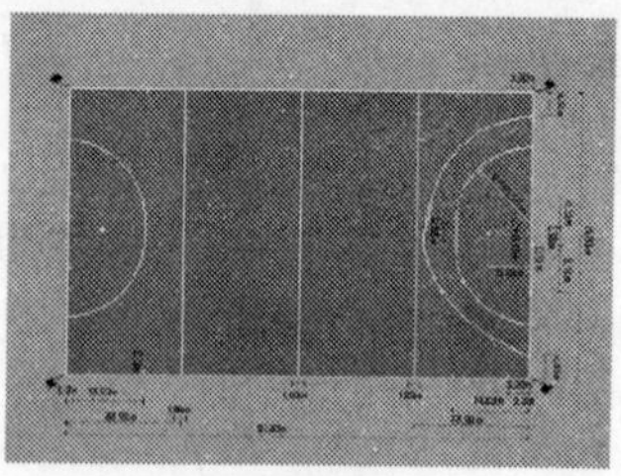

■ **pitch (rowing)**
the angle at which an oar is set in the water.

■ **pitch (rugby)**
the rugby field is a maximum of 100 meters long, from try-line to try-line and 70 metres wide. At each end of the field is an in-goal area, no more than 22 metres long. The field is marked by a half-way line, two 10-metre lines and two 22-metre lines and by two dotted hash marks, each 5 metres from the sideline and extending from goal-line to goal-line. There is a set of goal posts on each try-line.

■ **pitching rotation (baseball)**
the order in which the starting pitchers take turns starting games, usually with three or four days rest between starts.

■ **pitchout (baseball)**
when a pitch is thrown wide of the strike zone on purpose. A catcher will signal for a pitchout if they think that a runner is trying to steal.

■ **pitch-out (football)**
a lateral tossed from a quarterback to a running back.

■ **pivot (basketball)**
a centre; also the foot that must remain touching the floor until a ball handler who has stopped dribbling is ready to pass or shoot.

■ pixie gear (cycling)
same as *granny gear.*

■ place kick (rugby)
a kick made with the ball resting on the ground, in an indention in the ground, on a small pile of sand or on a kicking tee. A place kick is used for kickoffs, penalty kicks and conversion kicks.

■ place kick (football)
a kick towards the goalpost for a field goal or extra point; held between the ground and another player's finger.

■ placement (lawn tennis)
a shot hit to an area where the opponent cannot reach it.

■ planche (gymnastics)
a skill performed on the still rings in which the body is held in a straight position parallel to the floor above the rings.

■ plaque (fencing)
a point attack that lands flat.

■ plastron (fencing)
a partial jacket worn for extra protection; typically a half-jacket worn under the main jacket on the weapon-arm side of the body.

■ platform (weightlifting)
the competition area, 4 meters square and 50 to 150 millimetres high, where the competitors attempt their lifts. The platform may be made of any solid material such as wood or plastic and may be covered with a non-slippery material.

■ play clock (football)
a clock displayed above each end zone that limits the time teams may take between plays to 40 seconds (30 in college); the ball must be snapped before the clock runs down to 0.

■ play (football)
a spurt of action that begins with a snap and ends with a dead ball.

■ play-action pass (football)
a passing play after the quarterback has faked a hand-off.

■ playing surface (table tennis)
the table's upper surface.

■ playmaker (basketball)
the point guard who generally sets up plays for his teammates.

■ playoffs (football)
the post-season tournament that determines the NFL champion.

■ poach (lawn tennis)
in doubles, to hit a ball, usually with a volley that would ordinarily have been played by the partner.

■ pocket (football)
the area behind the offensive line, where the quarterback is protected by his blockers.

■ point (fencing)
a valid touch; the tip of the sword; the mechanical assembly that makes up the point of an electric weapon; an attack made with the point (i.e. a thrust).

■ point (lawn tennis)
the basic scoring unit in tennis. The points are numbered fifteen, thirty, forty and game. One player serves throughout a game and the first player to win four points wins the game, with the provision that the margin of victory must be at least two points. See advantage; deuce; game; match; set, scoring system.

■ point (table tennis)
a single scoring unit. A player loses a point if: He fails to make a good service or a good return of the opponent's shot; the ball bounces twice consecutively in his court; his free hand touches the playing surface. Points are also lost because of a double hit, obstruction or a volley.

■ point (water polo)
the offensive position farthest from the goal and ap-

proximately straight out from the goal.

■ point in line (fencing)

also line; an extended arm and blade that threatens the opponent.

■ point penalty (lawn tennis)

a penalty which costs the player a point in the current game. The umpire may assess a point penalty for various kinds of unsportsmanlike conduct, such as verbal or physical abuse of an official, using obscenity or delaying a game through incessant argument of a call.

■ point spread (basketball)

a device established by bookmakers to equalise 2 teams for betting purposes; e.g., if a team is considered to be 4 points better than another, the spread is 4 points; to win a bet on the favourite that team would need to win by more than the spread (in this case, by more than 4 points); the margin of victory can be more important than whether a team wins or loses.

■ point-after-touchdown (PAT) (football)

a place kick taken from the opponent's 2-yard line (3-yard line in college); awarded to a team that has scored a touchdown, it is worth 1 point if it goes through the goalpost.

■ points (icehockey)

the left and right positions taken by the defensemen of the attacking team, just inside the blue line of the attacking zone; also the term used to describe the defensemen playing at this location; also an individual statistic for players equal to their goals plus assists; also a team statistic used to determine team standings (2 points for each win and 1 point for each tie or overtime loss during the regular season).

■ points race (cycling)

this is similar to a scratch race, but points are awarded to the top riders in a series of sprints conducted at various points throughout the race and the winner is the rider who accumulates the most points.

■ **point-shaving (basketball)**
an illegal practice where players intentionally win a game, but by fewer points than the point spread; led to 2 major college scandals (involved 32 of the biggest stars in the 1950s, then 22 colleges in 1961).

■ **poke check (icehockey)**
a quick jab or thrust to the puck or opponent's stick to knock the puck away from him.

■ **pole line (cycling)**
a yellow line around the inside of a velodrome track that measures the track's length.

■ **policeman (icehockey)**
see *enforcer.*

■ **pommel (fencing)**
a fastener that attaches the grip to the blade.

■ **pommel horse (gymnastics)**
1. A piece of apparatus 115 centimetres high, 35 centimetres wide and 160 centimetres long, surmounted by two pommels, between 40 and 45 centimetres apart.
2. A men's event performed on the apparatus. A routine consists of a series of circular movements and required scissors elements performed with one or both hands on the pommels. No other part of the body may touch the apparatus.

■ **pop kick (rugby)**
a short, high kick, usually over the head of a nearby defender.

■ **port (rowing)**
the left side of a boat.

■ **port rig (rowing)**
an arrangement in which the stroke rows on the port side.

■ **possession (basketball)**
to be holding or in control of the ball.

■ **possession arrow (basketball)**
in college, used to determine which team's turn it is to inbounds the ball to begin a period or in a jump ball situation.

■ **possession (football)**
to be holding or in control of the football.

■ **post position (basketball)**
the position of a player standing in the low post or high post.

■ **power play (icehockey)**
an attack by a team at full strength against a team playing one man (or two men) shorthanded because of a penalty (or penalties) which resulted in a player on the opposing team receiving penalty-box time.

■ **power ten (rowing)**
a series of 10 powerful strokes, usually either to gain on a crew that's leading or to open a larger gap over a crew that's trailing.

■ **preparation (fencing)**
a non-threatening action intended to create the opening for an attack; the initial phase of an attack, before right-of-way is established.

■ **presentation (fencing)**
offering one's blade for engagement by the opponent.

■ **presentation (weightlifting)**
a ceremony held 15 minutes before the start of competition, at which the speaker introduces the technical officials and the athletes, who are lined up on the stage in the order of their start numbers.

■ press (fencing)
an attempt to push the opponent's blade aside or out of line; depending on the opponent's response, the press is followed by a direct or indirect attack.

■ press (water polo)
a defense that's extended beyond its normal range, designed to pressure offensive players into poor passes or shots.

■ press (weightlifting)
a lift in which the bar is brought to the shoulders and held there for two seconds while the lifter waits for approval from the chief referee. After approval, the bar is lifted overhead using only the arms. The press was one of three competitive lifts until 1976.

■ press-out (weightlifting)
an illegal move on which the lifter bends the arms while holding the bar overhead, then presses out to try to make them straight; results in no lift.

■ previous spot (football)
where the ball was snapped to begin the last play.

■ prime (fencing)
blade down and to the inside, wrist pronated.

■ principle of defence (fencing)
the use of forte against foible when parrying.

■ priority (fencing)
in sabre, the now-superceded rules that decide which fencer will be awarded the touch in the event that they both attack simultaneously; also used synonymously with right-of-way.

■ prise de fer (fencing)
also taking the blade; an engagement of the blades that forces the opponent's weapon into a new line. See (fencing) bind, croise, envelopment, opposition.

■ prix des nations (equestrian)
another name for the team show jumping event.

■ prop (rugby)
one of two forwards, who usually wear No. 1 (the loosehead prop) and No. 3 (The tighthead prop.) They support the hooker during scrums.

■ protection area (wrestling)
the border of the mat, extending at least 1.5 metres beyond the passivity zone, to help prevent injury if a wrestler is thrown outside the ring.

■ protocol (weightlifting)
the international weightlifting term for the scoresheet, on which the complete competition is recorded, including each successful and unsuccessful lift and totals for all competitors.

■ puck (icehockey)
a black, vulcanised rubber disc, 1-inch thick and 3-inches in diameter, weighing between 5 1/2 and 6 ounces used to play hockey; they are frozen to prevent excessive bouncing and changed throughout the game; can travel up to 120 miles per hour on a slap shot.

■ puddle (rowing)
the water movement caused by the action of the oars. The size and shape of the puddle are indications of the amount of power put into the stroke.

■ puddler (lawn tennis)
a player who hits a lot of chip shots and drop shots.

■ pull (cricket)
a hit executed by a batter pulling an off-side pitch around his body towards his other (i.e.on or leg) side.

■ pull (cycling)
to take a turn at the front of a pace line, thus pulling the other riders along.

■ pull (weightlifting)
the portion of the lift in which the bar is raised from the platform to the squat or split.

■ pull hitter (baseball)
a batter that generally hits to the same side of the field that he bats. (eg, righthanded pull

hitter hits to the left side of the field).

■ pulling the goalie (icehockey)
taking the goalkeeper off the ice and replacing him with a forward; leaves the goal unguarded so is only used as a last minute attempt to score.

■ punch volley (lawn tennis)
a volley hit with a very short, punching stroke.

■ punt (rugby)
a kick on which the ball is dropped and kicked before it reaches the ground. A goal cannot be scored with a punt.

■ punt (football)
when a player 10 yards behind the centre catches a snap, drops it and kicks it before it hits the ground; an opponent tries to catch and advance it the other way.

■ push (field hockey)
it is a push when a player moves the ball with a short, pushing movement of the stick, with both the ball and the head of the stick in contact with the ground.

■ push (table tennis)
a gentle shot with backspin, struck with an open paddle against the bottom of the ball and usually hit short and low.

■ push back (field hockey)
the centre pass.

■ push climb (cycling)
a portion of a trail where riders have to dismount and push or carry their bikes because of a very steep grade and/or poor traction.

■ push in (field hockey)
see *side in.*

■ push shot (badminton)
a soft shot on which the shuttlecock is gently pushed, with little or no wrist action. More commonly used in doubles than in singles.

■ **pushover try (rugby)**
a try that's scored by the pack in a scrumdown by pushing the opposition back across the goal line while dragging the ball along.

■ **put away (lawn tennis)**
same *as kill.*

■ **putout (baseball)**
in scoring, a fielder is credited with a putout if he receives the ball to put out a baserunner or a hitter.

■ **pylon (football)**
a short orange marker at each of the end zone's 4 corners.

■ **quadruple (rowing)**
a sculling boat for four rowers. Often shortened to quad.

■ **quadruple double (basketball)**
a triple double with double-digits scored in 4 categories.

■ **quarte (fencing)**
blade up and to the inside, wrist supinated.

■ **quarterback (football)**
the leader of a team's offense, he takes the snap from the centre and either hands the ball to a running back to run with, passes it to a receiver or runs with it himself; he also communicates each play to his teammates.

■ **quinte (fencing)**
blade up and to the inside, wrist pronated. In sabre, the blade is held above the head to protect from head cuts.

■ **race pace (rowing)**
a stroke rating that a crew can hold for an entire race.

■ **racing start (rowing)**
the opening strokes of a race, which are typically rowed at a high cadence to get the shell moving rapidly through the water.

■ **racket (badminton)**
the racketor bat, has a nearly round face, about 7 inches across and a long, thin handle. Overall length is about 27 inches and its weight is about 8 ounces.

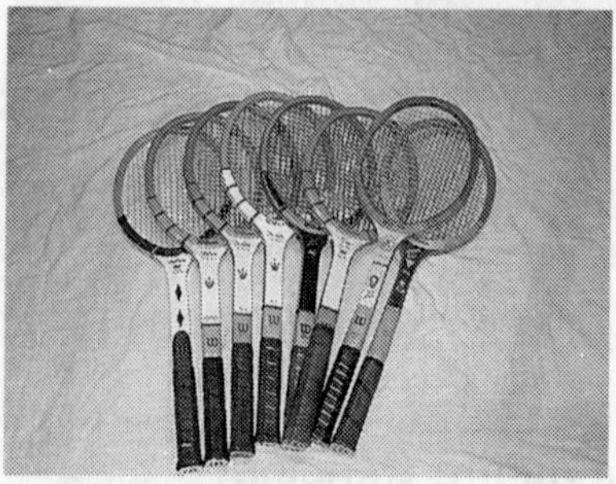

■ **racket (lawn tennis)**
the instrument that's used to hit the ball. It has a long, straight handle and an oval frame strung with natural gut or a synthetic material. Up until the late 1960s, rackets were made of wood, but then steel and aluminum frames were introduced, followed by frames of graphite, fibreglass, titanium and carbon. Maximum dimensions are 29 ½ inches in overall length, 12 ½ inches in overall width. The hitting surface can be no more than 15 ½ inches long and 11 ½ inches wide. Also spelled racquet.

■ **racket (table tennis)**
the paddle.

■ **ragging (icehockey)**
retaining the puck by clever stick handling; often used by a shorthanded team to kill time.

■ **rail (equestrian)**
a wooden bar or pole, as part of an obstacle.

■ **rainbow jersey (cycling)**
a multi-coloured striped jersey that is worn by the defending world champion.

■ **raised ball (field hockey)**
lifting the ball more than 18 inches above the ground with a hit is an offense, known as a raised ball, if it is dangerous or likely to lead to dangerous play.

■ **rally (badminton)**
an exchange of shots leading to a point or service change.

■ **rally (lawn tennis)**
an extended exchange of shots between players or sides.

■ **rally (table tennis)**
the period during which the ball is in play; an exchange of

shots that begins with a serve and ends with a point or a let.

■ **rapier (fencing)**
a long, double-edged thrusting sword popular in the 16th-17th centuries.

■ **rating (rowing)**
the number of strokes per minute a crew is rowing.

■ **reading the defense (football)**
recognition by the quarterback of the defensive formation; he may then call an audible to adjust the offense.

■ **ready position (lawn tennis)**
the position adopted by the receiver in anticipation of the serve.

■ **rebound (basketball)**
when a player grabs a ball that is coming off the rim or backboard after a shot attempt.

■ **rebound (icehockey)**
a puck that bounces off the goalie's body or equipment.

■ **receiver (basketball)**
the player who receives a pass from the ball handler.

■ **receiver (lawn tennis)**
the player who receives service throughout a game.

■ **receiver (table tennis)**
the player who is returning serve.

■ **receiver (football)**
an offensive player who catches or attempts to catch a forward pass.

■ **record board (weightlifting)**
a display that shows current records in the category being contested.

■ **recover (weightlifting)**
to return to a position with the legs side by side after a split.

■ **recovery (rowing)**
the portion of the stroke, between the release and the catch, during which the oar is brought into position for the next stroke.

■ recovery (football)
to gain or regain possession of a fumble.

■ red card (fencing)
used to indicate repeated minor rule infractions or a major rule infraction by one of the fencers; results in a point being given to the other fencer.

■ red card (field hockey)
if a player is guilty of an intentional foul, such as deliberate body contact or verbal abuse of officials, the referee issues a red card, which results in ejection from the game and suspension of the player for the team's next game.

■ red card (table tennis)
a card that calls for dismissal of an illegal advisor, when shown by the umpire. If shown along with a yellow card, it indicates that a penalty point has been awarded.

■ red line (icehockey)
the line that divides the length of the ice surface in half.

■ red shirt (football)
a designation given to a college player who did not play in any games during a particular year due to injury or coach's choice; such a player is permitted to practice with the team during that season and is granted an additional year of eligibility; most often used to describe college freshmen who are held out of games their first year to mature, becoming red shirt freshmen in their college.

■ red zone (football)
the imaginary area between the defense's 20-yard line and its goal line from which the offense is most likely to score points.

■ redoublement (fencing)
a new action that follows an attack that missed or was parried; renewal of a failed attack in the opposite line; alternatively see Reprise.

■ referee (fencing)
also director, president; the mediator of the fencing bout.

■ referee (lawn tennis)
the official who is in overall charge of a tournament. The referee doesn't officiate at matches, but may be called upon by the umpire to interpret a rule.

■ referee (rugby)
the sole judge and timekeeper for a match.

■ referee (water polo)
in major matches, there are two referees, one on each side of the pool. One is called the attacking or offensive referee, when the goal to his or her right is being attacked. The other, the defensive referee, remains at least as far back as the attacking player who is farthest from the goal. Referees together are responsible for calling fouls and declaring penalties.

■ referee (weightlifting)
there are three referees who rule on whether or not a lift is good, with the majority decision ruling. The chief referee signals the end of each lift by giving the lifter the down signal.

■ referee decision lights (weightlifting)
lights on the attempt board signal each referee's decision on whether or not a lift was valid. A white light indicates a good lift, a red light indicates no lift.

■ referee's crease (icehockey)
a semi-circular area, with a 10 foot radius, marked in red on the ice in front of the timekeepers' bench into which players may not follow a referee.

■ referees (icehockey)
the chief officials in a hockey game, distinguished from the other officials by a red armband; they start the game, call most of the penalties and make the final decision in any dispute; they are responsible for making sure the ice, the nets and the clock are in good condition; they wear black pants and an official

league sweater; they are also on skates.

■ **referee's position (wrestling)**
see *par terre.*

■ **refusal (equestrian)**
failure to jump a fence because the horse stops or tries to run around it. Scored as a disobedience.

■ **regatta (rowing)**
a boat race or a meeting at which a number of boat races take place.

■ **re-grasp (gymnastics)**
the act of grabbing the bar again after releasing from it.

■ **regulation game (basketball)**
four 12-minute quarters in the NBA or two 20-minute halves in college; a game that ends without overtime periods.

■ **rei (martial arts)**
bow; a command.

■ **reining (equestrian)**
a type of western riding in which the rider and horse perform an assigned pattern from memory, demonstrating various figures, stops and turns at varying speeds.

■ **release (basketball)**
the moment that the ball leaves a shooter's hands.

■ **release (rowing)**
the portion of the stroke when the oar is removed from the water.

■ **release (gymnastics)**
the act of leaving the bar and performing a move before the re-grasp.

■ **relief pitcher (baseball)**
the pitcher replacing the starting pitcher. The relief pitcher can win, lose, save or not be involved in the game's final score.

■ **remise (fencing)**
immediate replacement of an attack that missed or was parried, without withdrawing the arm.

■ **renwaku waza (martial arts)**
various techniques used in combination.

■ repechage (cycling)
a second chance given to losers of earlier heats in most match sprint competitions. The winner of a repechage continues on in the competition.

■ repechage (rowing)
a round of competition for boats that lost in a preliminary heat. Top finishers in a repechage continue to further rounds.

■ reprise (fencing)
renewal of an attack that missed or was parried, after a return to en-garde; alternatively.

■ resistance (equestrian)
acts by a horse that indicate a refusal to continue a round, such as rearing, making a half turnor stepping back.

■ restart (rugby)
the kickoff.

■ retreat (fencing)
step back; opposite of advance.

■ retrieve (lawn tennis)
to reach and return a shot that's difficult to get to.

■ retriever (lawn tennis)
a player who tries to wear down the opponent by concentrating on defense, continually chasing down and returning difficult shots.

■ return (lawn tennis)
to hit an opponent's shot back over the net and in play. After service, every successful shot is a return.

■ return (football)
an attempt by a player who has just caught an interception, puntor kickoff to advance the ball the other way.

■ reversal (wrestling)
if the wrestler in the bottom position completely reverses the situation and comes to the top position in control, it is a reversal, worth one point.

■ reverse spin (lawn tennis)
see *backspin.*

■ **reverse stick (field hockey)**
to turn the stick so that the blade points to the right, allowing a hit or push in that direction.

■ **reverse twist (lawn tennis)**
a serve that has spin causing it to bounce high and to receiver's right, off a right-handed player's racket. Opposite of American twist.

■ **ricasso (fencing)**
the portion of the tang between the grip and the blade, present on Italian hilts and most rapiers.

■ **riding time (wrestling)**
in high school and college wrestling, the amount of time a wrestler is in control of the opponent. One minute of riding time is worth a point.

■ **rig (rowing)**
the way in which riggers are arranged in a shell, which dictates how the oars and rowers are arranged. As a verb, to prepare a boat for racing. Also rigging.

■ **rigger (rowing)**
a device that connects the oarlock to the shell.

■ **right-of-way (fencing)**
rules for awarding the point in the event of a double touch in foil or sabre.

■ **rink (icehockey)**
the iced area inside the boards on which the game of hockey is played; it is 200 feet long by 85 feet wide with rounded corners.

■ **riposte (fencing)**
an offensive action made immediately after a parry of the opponent's attack.

■ **road rash (cycling)**
skin abrasion caused by a fall.

■ **roads and tracks (equestrian)**
two phases of the cross-country portion of the three-

day event, consisting of riding at a measured pace on the flat.

■ rockered blades (icehockey)

used by professional ice hockey skaters; the gentle curve in a very sharp blade of an ice skate produced by rounding the toe and heel of the blade to make it easier for hockey players to turn quickly.

■ roll back (equestrian)

a tight turn performed between two fences.

■ roll out (football)

when a quarterback runs parallel to the line, looking for a receiver.

■ rookie (basketball)

a player in his first NBA season.

■ rookie (football)

a first-year player in the NFL.

■ roster (basketball)

the list of players on a team.

■ rotation (badminton)

a system of playing doubles, used only by experts, in which the partners keep circling counterclockwise. Its chief advantage is that it virtually eliminates the backhand.

■ roughing (icehockey)

a minor penalty which occurs when a fight between players is more of a pushing and shoving match; a less severe penalty than fighting.

■ round (lawn tennis)

a series of matches in an elimination tournament, the winners of which advance to the next round.

■ round robin (lawn tennis)

a tournament in which each player meets every other

player and final standings are determined by the won-lost records. Such a tournament is sometimes a preliminary round to determine seedings and order of play.

■ roundoff (gymnastics)
a move similar to the cartwheel, with a half twist and the legs moving together.

■ routine (equestrian)
the series of movements a horse and rider follow in dressage.

■ routine (gymnastics)
a combination of moves and stunts displaying a full range of skills on the apparatus.

■ rowlock (rowing)
another name for the oarlock.

■ rubber (baseball)
a the pitching plate on the mound. The pitcher must have one foot connected to the plate while pitching to the batter. The rubber is located 60' 6 (19.5 metres) from home plate.

■ rubber sheet (table tennis)
a covering that's glued to the hitting side of a table tennis paddle, often over a thin layer of sponge. Many rubber sheets have pips on one side and are smooth on the other. See anti-spin rubber; combination paddle; hardbat; inverted rubber; long pips rubber; pips out; sandwich rubber; sticky rubber.

■ ruck (rugby)
when a runner has come into contact with opponents and the ball has gone to the ground, players may bind themselves into a ruck. There must be at least three players bound. The ruck ends when the ball leaves the ruck and can be handled by a player who is not part of the ruck or when a scrum is ordered. A ruck is similar to a maul, except that the ball is on the ground.

■ rudder (rowing)
a small fin that allows the coxswain to steer the boat.

■ **rudder cable (rowing)**
a rope or cable operated by the coxswain to turn the rudder.

■ **rugger (rugby)**
a rugby player.

■ **run (basketball)**
occurs when one team scores several field goals in quick succession while its opponents score few or none.

■ **run (rowing)**
the distance a boat travels during one stroke.

■ **run around the backhand (lawn tennis)**
to make excessive movement in order to play a ball on the forehand rather than on the backhand.

■ **run batter in (rbi) (baseball)**
statistics which shows how often a player has made it possible for his/her team mates to score while at bat. A player who has 30 RBI's has caused 30 runs to be score. A batter is not credited with an RBI if he hits into a double play or if the run is scored because of an error.

■ **run down (lawn tennis)**
same as retrieve.

■ **run down (baseball)**
a played used by fielders to tag out a runner caught between bases.

■ **run out see pic above (cricket)**
like baseball's tag.an out which consists of the fielder striking the wickets towards which a runner is headed, before he gets to it.

■ **run rate (cricket)**
the rate at which runs are being scored per over, in an innings.

■ **run (baseball)**
score obtained when a base runner safely crosses home plate.

■ **run (s) (cricket)**
safe crossing (s) from wicket to wicket, by a batter (and his partner) after hitting (earned runs)or off a fielding error (like stolen bases) (extras).

Each crossing scores one run to the batting team.

■ **runback (lawn tennis)**
the area between the baseline and the backstop.

■ **runner (baseball)**
an offensive player who is advancing toward, touching or returning to any base.

■ **run-out (equestrian)**
an attempt by the horse the escape the rider's control in order to avoid jumping an obstacle.

■ **run-up (equestrian)**
the short burst of speed put on by a horse in order to clear a jump.

■ **rush (icehockey)**
an individual or combined attack by a team in possession of the puck.

■ **rush the slide (rowing)**
to move from the recovery to the catch too quickly, often the result of a lunge.

■ **rush (football)**
a running play; also, a pass rush.

■ **sabre (fencing)**
a fencing weapon with a flat blade and knuckle guard, used with cutting or thrusting actions; a military sword popular in the 18th to 20th centuries; any cutting sword used by cavalry.

■ **sack (football)**
a tackle of the quarterback behind his line of scrimmage.

■ **sacrifice bunt (baseball)**
a bunt designed to advance a runner although the batter will be thrown out.

■ **sacrifice fly (baseball)**
fly ball out that scores a runner from third base.

■ **safe (baseball)**
declaration by the umpire that a runner is entitled to the bases for which he was trying.

■ safety cup (equestrian)
a cup used on the back rail of a spread fence that releases to drop the rail if struck by the horse.

■ safety (football)
when a ball carrier is tackled in his own end zone after bringing the ball there under his own power; the defense earns 2 points and receives a free kick from the offense's own 20-yard line.

■ salary cap (basketball)
an annual dollar limit that a single team may pay all its players.

■ salle (fencing)
a fencing hall or club.

■ salto (gymnastics)
an aerial flip or somersault in which the feet come up over the head and the body rotates around the waist.

■ salute (fencing)
with the weapon, a customary acknowledgement of one's opponent and referee at the start and end of the bout.

■ sandwich rubber (table tennis)
a rubber sheet attached to the paddle with an underlying layer of sponge.

■ save (icehockey)
the act of a goalie in blocking or stopping a shot.

■ save (baseball)
a relief pitcher can be credited with a save if they can keep the team's lead while the opponent's tying or winning runs are on base or if they pitch 3 or more innings without allowing the opponents to tie the game.

■ schlager (fencing)
German fraternity duelling sword, used with cuts to the face and no footwork.

■ **schooling (equestrian)**
training in preparation for competition.

■ **schooling area (equestrian)**
an area in which horses can be warmed up before a jumping competition.

■ **scoop (field hockey)**
it is a scoop when a player raises a stationary or slowly moving ball off the ground with a shovel-like movement of the stick, which is placed slightly under the ball.

■ **scoresheet (weightlifting)**
see *protocol.*

■ **scoring opportunity (basketball)**
when a player gets open for a shot that is likely to score.

■ **scoring position (baseball)**
runner on second or third base.

■ **scoring system (lawn tennis)**
the scoring system for modern tennis is based on that of its medieval ancestor, court tennis. In court tennis, a game comprised four rounds of 15 points each. That system was imposed on lawn tennis, as it used to be known, with the points numbered 15, 30, 45and 60 (or game). Somewhere along the line, 45 was abbreviated to 40. The point is the basic building block; a game is made up of points, a set is made up of games and a match is made up of sets.

■ **scramble (icehockey)**
several players from both sides close together battling for possession of the puck.

■ **scrambling (football)**
evasive movements by a quarterback to avoid being sacked.

■ **scratch race (cycling)**
any race in which all riders cover the same distance from a mass start and the winner is the first rider across the finish line. Virtually all road races are scratch races.

■ screen or screener (basketball)
the offensive player who stands between a teammate and a defender to gives his teammate the chance to take an open shot.

■ screen shot (icehockey)
a shot on goal that the goalie cannot see because it was taken from behind one or more players from either team standing in front of the net.

■ scrum (rugby)
a formation used to restart play after a knock-on or forward pass or at any time when ordered by the referee. Forwards on each side bind and the two groups come together, with the front rows interlocking to leave a tunnel between them. The scrumhalf of the non-offending team feeds the ball into the tunnel from 1 metre away, midway between the front rows. The hookers attempt to get the ball out to a back. The scrum ends when the ball is out of the tunnel and in possession of a player on either team.

■ scrumdown (rugby)
the process of bringing a scrum together.

■ scrumhalf (rugby)
the back, usually No. 9, who feeds the ball into the scrum and tries to retrieve the ball from mauls, rucks and scrums. Also called the half-back.

■ scrummage (rugby)
the entire process of setting and completing a scrum.

■ scull (rowing)
one of a pair of oars that are used by a single rower, one in each hand. As a verb, to use sculls to propel a boat.

■ seamer (cricket)
a faster pitch delivered with the seam straight and which can slide in the air or break unexpectedly.

■ seat (rowing)
a platform of plastic or wood that sits on the slides and moves back and forth with the rower's motion.

Seats are numbered from bow to stern and rowers are often identified by their seat numbers. In an eight, the bowman is No. 1 and the stroke is No. 8.

■ second 5/8th (rugby)
another name for a centre.

■ second flight (lawn tennis)
the flight of the ball after it bounces.

■ second intention (fencing)
a false action used to draw a response from the opponent, which will open the opportunity for the intended action that follows, typically a counter-riposte.

■ second row (rugby)
the two locks, when in a scrum.

■ seconde (fencing)
blade down and to the outside, wrist pronated.

■ seed (lawn tennis)
before a tournament, certain players are ranked, based on their ability and recent performances. The process is called seeding, the rankings are called seeds and the top-ranked player is called the top seed. Matches are then arranged so that the top-seeded players will not meet until the later rounds of the tournament.

■ Seemiller grip (table tennis)
a grip in which a combination paddle is constantly rotated so that the ball can be struck with either side of the hitting surface.

■ sendoff (rugby)
the expulsion of a player from a match. The side has to play one person short and the player sent off is typically banned for at least one further match. A sendoff may result from a flagrant or malicious foul or from repeated fouls.

■ sensei (martial arts)
a teacher; literally one who has been born before, therefore an elder.

■ sensei-ni (martial arts)
face toward the instruct or; a command.

■ septime (fencing)
blade down and to the inside, wrist supinated.

■ series (football)
the group of 4 downs a team has to advance 10 yards.

■ serve (lawn tennis)
the shot that begin each point. Standing behind the baseline, the player must toss the ball into the air and hit it into the diagonally opposite service court. The server is given two chances to make a valid serve. A failure is called a fault and a double fault results in loss of the point. On the first point, the server must be to the right of the centre line and then alternates sides with each point. In singles, the players alternate service throughout a match. In doubles, service alternates between the sides and all four players serve in turn.

■ serve (table tennis)
short for service.

■ serve and volley (lawn tennis)
a style of play in which the server takes the net after each successful serve in order to volley the opponent's return.

■ server (lawn tennis)
the player whose turn it is to serve.

■ server (table tennis)
the player who strikes the ball first in a rally.

■ service (lawn tennis)
see *serve.*

■ service (table tennis)
the shot that starts a rally. The server must toss the ball up at least 16 centimetres (6 inches) and strike it as it's falling, so that it touches first in the server's court and then in the receiver's court, without touching the net. When struck, the ball must be above the level of the playing surface and behind the server's end line. See also let.

■ **service court (lawn tennis)**
one of the two rectangles on each side of the net bounded by the service sideline, the service line, the centre service line between them and the net itself. Each service court is 21 feet deep and 13 ½ feet wide.

■ **service line (lawn tennis)**
the line that marks the back boundary of the service courts on each side of the net.

■ **service line judge (lawn tennis)**
an official who is responsible for determining whether a serve hits the court beyond the service line. The service line judges are stationed on the same side of the court as the umpire and on a line with the service lines.

■ **service sideline (lawn tennis)**
that part of the singles sideline, between the net and the service linethat marks the outside boundary of the service court.

■ **service winner (lawn tennis)**
a serve that the receiver hits without making a legal return.

■ **set (lawn tennis)**
a set is a group of games that is won by the player or side that first wins at least six games with a two-game margin, unless a tie-breaker is employed. In major tournaments, there are usually five sets in a men's match and three in a women's match.

■ **set (rowing)**
the boat's balance, a delicate property that's affected by the posture and timing of the rowers as well as by qualities of the boat itself.

■ **set point (lawn tennis)**
a point that, if won by the leader, will result in winning the set.

■ **seven-metre line (water polo)**
an imaginary line extending across the pool, seven metres from each goal line.

■ **sevens (rugby)**
a version of rugby with only seven players on a side, typically three forwards and four backs. A half is usually only seven minutes long.

■ **shakehand grip (table tennis)**
a grip in which the paddle is held as if the player were shaking hands with it.

■ **shell (rowing)**
a racing boat.

■ **shiai (martial arts)**
a contest.

■ **shido (martial arts)**
a minor violation that gives the opponent a koka. If a similar violation is committed later in the match, the shido is increased to a chui. (Judo).

■ **shihan (martial arts)**
a master instructor.

■ **shime waza (martial arts)**
strangling and choking techniques.

■ **shinai (martial arts)**
a bamboo sword used in kendo.

■ **shodan (martial arts)**
a first degree black belt.

■ **shooter (basketball)**
a player who takes a shot at the basket.

■ **shooter's roll (basketball)**
the ability to get even an inaccurate shot to bounce lightly off the rim and into the basket.

■ **shooting angle (icehockey)**
the angle determined by the position of the shooting player in relation to the goal at the moment he shoots the puck.

■ **shooting circle (field hockey)**
see *goal circle*.

■ **shooting range (basketball)**
the distance from which a player is likely to make his shots.

shootout (water polo)
see penalty shootout.

shorthanded (icehockey)
a team with one or more players off the ice in the penalty box when the opponent has its full complement of 6 players; also a power play for the other team.

shortstop (baseball)
defensive player positioned between second and third bases.

shot (lawn tennis)
the act of hitting the ball with the racket.

shot clock (basketball)
a clock that limits the time a team with the ball has to shoot it; 24 seconds in the NBA; in college, 35 seconds for men, 30 seconds for women.

shot clock (water polo)
a clock which displays the time remaining for a team to take a shot. Also known as possession clock.

shot on goal (sog) (icehockey)
a scoring attempt that would enter the goal if not stopped by a goalie (icehockey) results in either a goal or a save.

shoulder deke (icehockey)
a quick move of the shoulder in one direction and the player in another to fake out the opponent.

show jumping (equestrian)
an event in which the horse must clear a number of obstacles on a set course within a specified time.

shut out (baseball)
a game in which one team doesn't score any runs.

shuto uke (martial arts)
blocks in which the edge of the hand is used.

■ shuttlecock (badminton)
the shuttlecock, also known as the shuttle or bird, is a hemisphere of cork, 1 to 1 $^{1}/_{8}$ inches in diameter, surmounted by a short cylindrical crown in which are embedded 14 to 16 feathers, 2 $^{1}/_{4}$ to 2 $^{3}/_{4}$ inches long, with a toop spread of from 2 $^{1}/_{8}$ to 2 $^{1}/_{2}$ inches. The weight is between 73 and 85 grains (about 1 $^{1}/_{6}$ ounce).

■ side in (field hockey)
a pass that puts the ball back into play after it has gone out of bounds. Also known as a push in.

■ side line (table tennis)
one of the two white lines marking the side edges of the table.

■ sideboards (icehockey)
the boards along the sides of the rink.

■ side-by-side (badminton)
a doubles formation in which each partner is responsible for one side of the court.

■ sideline (lawn tennis)
the line that marks the side boundary of the court. The sidelines are 27 feet apart for singles and 36 feet apart for doubles.

■ sideline judge (lawn tennis)
an official who is responsible for determining whether a shot lands outside the sideline or in the court. There are four sideline judges, two at each end of the court.

■ sideline (football)
the boundary line that runs the length of the field along each side; a ball carrier or ball that touches or crosses the sideline is out of bounds.

■ sidelines (basketball)
2 boundary lines that run the length of the court.

sidespin (lawn tennis)
spin around the ball's vertical axis, applied by drawing the racket strings horizontally across the ball at the moment of contact.

sidespin (table tennis)
spin around the ball's vertical axis, imparted by drawing the paddle sideways across the ball at impact.

signs (baseball)
1. Player signals given from the third base coach to the hitter and runner. 2. Hand signals given by the catcher to the pitcher suggesting the type of pitch to be thrown.

simple (fencing)
executed in one movement; an attack or riposte that involves no feints.

simple grip (weightlifting)
a grip in which all four fingers of the hand are on one side of the bar and the thumb is on the other side.

simultaneous (fencing)
in foil and sabre, two attacks for which the right-of-way is too close to determine.

single (rowing)
a sculling boat for one rower.

single stick (fencing)
an archaic form of fencing with basket-hilted wooden sticks.

single track (cycling)
a section of trail that's wide enough for only one rider.

single-elimination (football)
a tournament where a team is eliminated after one loss.

single-leg tackle (wrestling)
a move in which a wrestler takes the opponent down by lifting one of the opponent's legs.

singles (lawn tennis)
a match between two players.

singles (table tennis)
competition between two individuals.

■ singles court (lawn tennis)
the court used for a singles match, which is 27 feet wide.

■ singles sideline (lawn tennis)
one of the two lines that mark the side boundaries of the singles court.

■ singlet (wrestling)
the one-piece uniform worn by wrestlers. One wrestler wears red, the other blue.

■ single-time (fencing)
also stesso tempo; parry-riposte as a single action.

■ sink (water polo)
to push an opposing player under the water.

■ sinker (baseball)
a fast pitch that breaks downward as it reaches.

■ sit in (cycling)
to get close behind the rider immediately in front in order to draft.

■ six for six (weightlifting)
the feat of making good lifts in all six attempts, three in the snatch and three in the clean and jerk.

■ sixer or over-boundary (cricket)
a hit that flies over the fence without a bounce, scoring six runs.

■ sixte (fencing)
blade up and to the outside, wrist supinated.

■ sixteen-yard hit (field hockey)
when the offense commits a foul in the goal circle, the opponent is given a free hit at the top of the circle, 16 yards from the end line.

■ sixth man (basketball)
the best substitute on a team; usually the first player to come off the bench to replace a starter.

■ skeg (rowing)
a small, flat piece of wood or plastic attached perpendicularly to the bottom of the shell to help hold it on a straight course; also known as the fin.

■ skying (rowing)
a poor rowing technique in which the blade is too high

above the surface of the water at the catch.

■ **slam (wrestling)**
to lifting the opponent from the mat and bring him back down with unnecessary force; illegal in amateur wrestling.

■ **slam dunk (basketball)**
see *dunk*.

■ **slap shot (icehockey)**
a shot in which the player raises his stick in a backswing, with his strong hand held low on the shaft and his other hand on the end as a pivot. Then as the stick comes down toward the puck, the player leans into the stick to put all his power behind the shot and add velocity to the puck; achieves an extremely high speed (up to 120 miles per hour) but is less accurate than a wrist shot.

■ **slashing (icehockey)**
a minor penalty which occurs when a player swings his stick hard at an opponent, whether or not contact is made; if injury is caused it becomes a major penalty and a game misconduct.

■ **sleeper (icehockey)**
an attacking player who slips into the centre or neutral zone behind the attacking defensemen; same as a floater or a hanger.

■ **sleeve (weightlifting)**
one of the two end portions of the bar, where the weights are attached.

■ **slice (lawn tennis)**
a shot hit with both backspin and sidespin; as a verb, to hit such a shot.

■ **slide (rowing)**
a set of runners holding wheels for each seat in a boat.

■ **slider (baseball)**
a pitcher that appears to the batter as a fastball until it reaches the plate, then breaks sharply on a level plane. The ball is held similarly to the curveball, but the wrist is kept straight, like a fastball and broken downward.

■ **sliding stop (equestrian)**
a stop in which the horse balances on the back feet while continuing to move the front feet.

■ **sling (badminton)**
see *carry.*

■ **slipstream (cycling)**
the area of lowered wind resistance behind a rider.

■ **slow whistle (icehockey)**
when an official waits to blow his whistle because of a delayed offside or delayed penalty call.

■ **small sword (fencing)**
a light duelling sword popular in the 17th-18th centuries, precursor to the foil.

■ **smash (badminton)**
an overhand shot on which the shuttle travels sharply downward.

■ **smash (lawn tennis)**
an overhead shot that is hit very hard and down into the opponent's side of the net.

■ **smash (table tennis)**
a kill.

■ **smythe division (icehockey)**
with the Norris Division made up the Campbell Conference until the 1992-93 season; renamed the Pacific Division of the Western Conference starting with the 1993-94 season.

■ **snakebite (cycling)**
same as *pinch flat.*

■ **snap volley (lawn tennis)**
a volley given extra velocity by wrist action at impact.

■ **snap (football)**
when the centre while facing forward quickly hands the ball between his legs to a player standing behind him (usually the quarterback) to start each play.

■ snatch (weightlifting)
a lift in which the bar is brought from the platform to an overhead position in one continuous motion, while splitting or squatting and then straightening to an upright position. The lifter must hold the bar overhead, with arms straight, until the referee gives the down signal.

■ sogo gachi (martial arts)
a compound win that results when the combatant has a waza-ari and the opponent is penalised with a keikoku. (Judo).

■ solo (icehockey)
a rush by a player without assistance from a teammate.

■ somi-and-a-half (gymnastics)
a one and a half somersault.

■ spacing (rowing)
same as run.

■ speaker (weightlifting)
the official who moderates the competition, announcing the name of the athlete about to attempt a lift and announcing the validity or nonvalidity of the lift after it has been attempted. The speaker also introduces the athletes and other officials during the presentation.

■ spearing (icehockey)
a major penalty which occurs when a player illegally jabs or even just attempts to jab, the point of his stick blade into another player's body; one of the most serious infractions a player can commit; results in an automatic game misconduct.

■ special teams (football)
the group of players who participate in kicking plays.

■ spectacles (cricket)
a double duck, i.e. a batter who is out for zero runs in both innings of a two-inning cricket game.

■ speed and endurance (equestrian)
the second day's portion of the three-day event, consisting of roads and tracks, steeplechase and the cross country obstacle course. Also known as the cross-country section.

■ spike (football)
when a player throws the ball at the ground to celebrate a touchdown.

■ spin (bowler) (cricket)
a kind of pitch, usually delivered at slow speed, where fingers or/and wrist are used to impart spin to the ball to achieve breaks so, spin bowler is a pitcher who uses spin.

■ spin (cycling)
to pedal at a very high cadence.

■ spiral (football)
a ball passed or kicked with a spin which propels it further with more accuracy; the ball points the same direction throughout its flight.

■ spit ball (baseball)
illegal pitch which a foreign substance (most commonly spit or grease) is applied to the ball causing it to react in an unpredictable manner.

■ splashing (water polo)
deliberately splashing water in an opponent's face is an exclusion foul.

■ split (weightlifting)
to bend one leg forward, the other straight back, while lowering the body toward the floor.

■ sponge (table tennis)
a thin layer of sponge rubber attached between the rubber sheet and the blade to increase speed and spin.

■ spot (football)
a location on the field, determined by an official, to mark forward progress or the place of a foul.

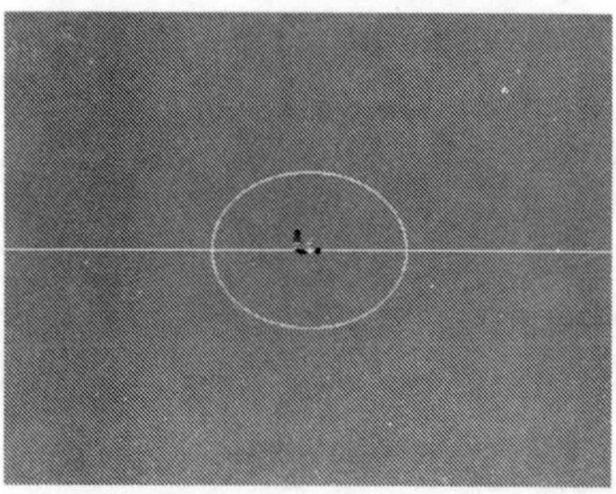

■ sprawl (wrestling)
a move used to counter a leg shot. The wrestler throws the legs back and arches the hips into the opponent to break the hold.

■ spread (equestrian)
an obstacle that combines width and height, requiring the horse to jump horizontally as well as vertically.

■ sprint (rowing)
1) The last 500 meters of a 2,000-meter race. 2) A race substantially shorter than 2,000 meters.

■ sprint (water polo)
see *swim-off.*

■ spur (equestrian)
a pointed device on the rider's boot heel, used to urge a horse forward.

■ square (rowing)
to turn the oar's blade so it's perpendicular to the surface of the water. The blade is squared at the end of recovery, in preparation for the catch.

■ square cut (cricket)
a hit that looks like a slash across the body, used by batter to hit the ball square to his batting position.in baseball terms, like a hit towards first base by a right-handed batter or third base by a left-hander.

■ squaring up (basketball)
when a player's shoulders are facing the basket as he releases the ball for a shot; considered good shooting position.

■ squat (weightlifting)
to bend the legs at the knees while lowering the body toward the floor.

■ stalling (water polo)
failing to shoot or advance the ball within 35 seconds. An ordinary foul.

■ standing position (wrestling)

see *neutral position.*

■ starboard (rowing)

the right side of a boat.

■ start number (weightlifting)

a number given to indicate a competitor's place in the starting order. Within each group, starting numbers are based on lot numbers; that is, the competitors with the lowest lot number is given No. 1 and so on.

■ starter (baseball)

the pitcher who beings the game and pitches until he wins the game or is replaced by a relief pitcher.

■ starting dock (rowing)

a dock at the start line where the boats are aligned before the race.

■ starting lineup (basketball)

the 5 starters who begin a game; usually a team's best players.

■ stationary pick (water polo)

a move in which an offensive player stops in front of a player who is defending another offensive player, freeing that teammate to receive a pass or take a shot.

■ steal (baseball)

attempting to advance a base between pitches without the batter hitting the ball or getting a base on balls.

■ steeplechase (equestrian)

a phase of the speed and endurance portion of the three-day event, in which the horses run over a turf track with several low fences.

■ stern (rowing)

the back part of a boat.

■ stick (field hockey)

the field hockey stick is made of wood or fibreglass and has a curved head that is flat on one side and rounded on the other. Only the flat side of the stick can be used to strike the ball.

■ **stick deke (icehockey)**
when a player's stick is moved as though for a shot, but instead the player moves the puck past the defending player; done to fake out the opponent.

■ **stick interference (field hockey)**
using the stick to hit an opponent's stick, whether intentionally or unintentionally.

■ **stick (gymnastics)**
to land a dismount or final move without taking additional steps.

■ **stickhandling (icehockey)**
moving the puck along the ice with the stick blade.

■ **sticky rubber (table tennis)**
a type of rubber that allows the player to put a lot of spin on the ball.

■ **sticky wicket (cricket)**
a field which is partly dry and partly wet, creating a treacherous and uncertain bounce which makes the batter's life difficult by extrapolation, any life situation which is full of hazardous uncertainty!

■ **stiff arm (or straight arm) (football)**
a push by a ball carrier to ward off a tackler.

■ **still rings (gymnastics)**
1) A piece of apparatus consisting of a tower, 575 centimetres high, from which two rings are suspended by a cable and straps. The cable and straps are 300 centimeters long and 50 centimetres apart. 2) A men's event performed on the apparatus. A routine includes a series of swings and holds, finishing with an acrobatic dismount. The rings must remain absolutely still and in the gymnast's control at the conclusion of each skill.

■ **stirrup (equestrian)**
a loop or ring hung from the saddle that supports the rider's foot.

■ **stock seat (equestrian)**
a division of western riding, in which the rider manoeuvers the horse through livestock that are to be controlled, moved or roped.

■ **stolen base (baseball)**
successfully advancing a base between pitches without the batter hitting the ball or getting a base on balls.

■ **stonewall (cricket)**
to bat only to stop the pitcher from hitting the sticks, without attempting to score. A defensive tactic, like basketball's stall.

■ **stop cut (fencing)**
a stop-hit with the edge in sabre, typically to the cuff.

■ **stop hit (fencing)**
a counter-attack that hits; also a counter-attack whose touch is valid by virtue of its timing.

■ **stop the rot (cricket)**
bat in a partnership that lasts long enough and scores enough runs to make up for a succession of quick outs and a low score total, earlier in the innings.

■ **stop volley (lawn tennis)**
a volley, hit with little motion of the racket that drops just over the net.

■ **straddle split (gymnastics)**
a split in the straddle position.

■ **straddle swing (gymnastics)**
a swing movement in which the legs are extended to each side.

■ **straddle (gymnastics)**
a position in which the legs are spread far apart to the side.

■ **straight sets (lawn tennis)**
descriptive of a match in which one player wins all the sets.

■ stretcher (rowing)
a set of two inclined foot rests that hold each rower's shoes.

■ striding (equestrian)
a single, coordinated movement of all four of the horse's legs, after which the legs return to their starting position.

■ strike out (baseball)
out recorded by recording three strikes on the batter.

■ strike rate (cricket)
the number of earned runs scored by a batter per pitches actually faced by him.

■ strike zone (baseball)
the area over home plate between the batter's armpits and knees when the batter is positioned to swing. Any pitch that is delivered through this area is called a strike.

■ strike (baseball)
a strike is called if a batter swings at a pitch and misses or if the pitch simply passes through the strike zone. The first 2 foul balls that are not caught count as first and second strike. A foul ball that is not caught can never be counted as a third strike.

■ striking circle (field hockey)
see *goal circle.*

■ strings (lawn tennis)
the hitting surface of the racket, made up of interlaced strings of gut or synthetic material.

■ stroke (lawn tennis)
a swing at the ball; a shot.

■ stroke (rowing)
1. The total rowing motion, including catch, drive, finish, release and recovery.
2. The rower nearest the stem, who sets the cadence for the rest of the crew.

■ stroke counter (table tennis)
an official who counts return strokes when the expedite system is in effect.

■ strong side (water polo)
the side of the pool on which the ball is located.

■ stumped (cricket)
an out which is made by the catcher/wicket-keeper, catching the batter out of his ground when he is trying to hit.and misses.

■ submission (equestrian)
unresisting obedience to the rider.

■ substitute (basketball)
a player who comes into the game to replace a player on the court.

■ substitution (icehockey)
occurs when a player comes off the bench to replace a player coming out of the game; can be made at any time and play does not need to stop.

■ succeeding spot (football)
where the next play would start if no penalty was called.

■ sudden death (lawn tennis)
a tie-breaker of predetermined length. The most commonly used are the 9-point tie-breaker, in which the first player to score 5 points is the winner and the 13-point tie-breaker, which is won by the first player to score 7 points.

■ sudden-death overtime (icehockey)
an overtime period that ends as soon as one team scores a goal, determining the winner and terminating the game.

■ suicide squeeze play (baseball)
a play in which a runner on third breaks toward home on the pitch and the batter's responsibility is to bunt the ball allowing the runner to score.

■ **Super Bowl (football)**
the championship game of the NFL, played between the champions of the AFC and NFC at a neutral site. It is the culmination of the NFL playoffs.

■ **suspension (cycling)**
a system that absorbs shock on mountain bikes and some road bikes.

■ **sutemi waza (martial arts)**
sacrifice techniques, in which the defender apparently yields to the attacker's pressure and then uses the attacker's momentum to execute a throw.

■ **swedish fall (gymnastics)**
a drop straight to the ground in which the hands shoot out an instant before landing.

■ **sweep (cricket)**
a hit executed towards his leg or on side, by sweeping his bat around his body.

■ **sweep (martial arts)**
a method of bringing an opponent down by knocking one of his legs out of its stance and then throwing him off balance.

■ **sweep (rowing)**
the oar used in a sweep-oared boat; as an adjective, descriptive of the boat itself.

■ **sweep check (icehockey)**
a check made by a player with one hand on the stick and one knee so low it is practically on the ice, with the shaft and blade of the stick flat on the ice to take the puck away from an opponent.

■ **sweep-oar rowing (rowing)**
rowing with a single oar, gripped by both hands.

■ **sweet spot (lawn tennis)**
the optimum hitting area, around the middle of the racket face.

■ **swim-off (water polo)**
the method of starting a period. Players take up positions on their own goal lines. A referee then blows the whistle, tosses the ball into the centre of the pool and

the players race for it. Also called a sprint.

■ **swing man (basketball)**
a player who can play both the guard and forward positions.

■ **switch-hitter (baseball)**
player who is able to bat left-handed or right-handed. A switch-hitter will bat from the opposite side in which the pitchers throws.

■ **T (lawn tennis)**
the midcourt area, where the service lines meet the centre service line.

■ **table (table tennis)**
the table must be 9 feet long and 5 feet wide, with the surface 30 inches above the floor.

■ **tack (equestrian)**
riding equipment. Short for tackle.

■ **tackle (field hockey)**
an attempt to take the ball away from the opponent, using the stick.

■ **tackle (rugby)**
the act of grabbing a player who has the ball and bringing him to the ground.

■ **tackle (football)**
a player position on both the offensive and defensive lines; there is usually a left and right offensive tackle and a left and right defensive tackle; See also *tackling*.

■ **tackling (football)**
contacting a ball carrier to cause him to touch the ground with any part of his body except his hands, thereby ending the play.

■ **tae kwon do (martial arts)**
a Korean martial art, featuring punches and kicks, which

became an Olympic sport in 2000. Often spelled as one word. Literally, the way of hand and foot.

■ **tag (baseball)**
1. An action runners must perform before they can advance on a fly ball. Runners must touch the base they occupy after the ball is caught before they can try to advance. Runners can leave their base before a ball it hit, but must return and touch the base if the ball is caught. 2. An action executed when a defensive player touches a runner with the ball in an attempt to get them out.

■ **t'ai chi ch'uan (martial arts)**
usually known simply as tai chi, this Chinese martial art emphasises slow, smooth movements and is commonly practiced to improve self-control and teach calmness. However, it does also have martial applications.

■ **tail-ender (cricket)**
the last to or three batters in a team's batting order. The tail wags if these batters manage to score a significant amount of runs!

■ **take (rugby)**
a good catch of a kick.

■ **take a flyer (cycling)**
see *flyer*.

■ **take guard (cricket)**
what a batter does when he first goes in to bat, i.e. he asks the umpire for guidance and marks his position where he wishes to stand when batting.

■ **take the net (lawn tennis)**
to move into the forecourt and toward the net in order to be able to hit volleys into

the opponent's side of the court.

■ **takedown (wrestling)**
when a wrestler takes the opponent to the mat from the neutral position, it is a takedown, worth one point.

■ **take-off point (equestrian)**
the best point at which a horse should jump in order to clear an obstacle.

■ **tandem (lawn tennis)**
a doubles formation in which each partner is responsible for one half of the court, as divided by the centre line. Compare *up and back*.

■ **tandem rig (rowing)**
a rowing arrangement in which each set of two adjacent riggers is on the same side of the boat.

■ **tandem sprint (cycling)**
the tandem sprint is like a match sprint, but it's ridden on two-man tandem bicycles over a 1,500-metre course.

■ **tape (lawn tennis)**
the band of white canvas or synthetic material, 2 to 2 ½ inches wide that covers the top of the net.

■ **tap-penalty (rugby)**
a penalty kick on which the player taps the ball with the foot, then picks it up and passes it to a teammate.

■ **tatami (martial arts)**
the mat that marks the competition area in judo, usually made of pressed foam and 16 square meters in area.

■ **te waza (martial arts)**
techniques of using the hand to counter or deliver blows.

■ **team (water polo)**
a team is made up of seven players, including a goalkeeper and a maximum of six substitutes.

■ team fouls (basketball)
each personal foul committed by a player is also counted against his team; when a team goes over the limit, its opponent is awarded free-throw opportunities.

■ team pursuit (cycling)
this is similar to the individual pursuit race, except that there are two teams of four riders each. The teams ride in pace lines and the leader changes every half-lap or every lap. Standard distance is 4,000 metres. The team's time is taken when the third rider crosses the finish line, so the fourth rider doesn't have to finish.

■ team tennis (lawn tennis)
a type of competition between teams of players, involving singles and doubles matches, in which the victory is the team that takes the most games.

■ technical (cycling)
descriptive of a portion of trail that tests a rider's handling skills.

■ technical controller (weightlifting)
one of two officials at each competition who are responsible for examining the athletes and their outfits, keeping track of the starting order and the progression of weights and other similar tasks.

■ technical fall (wrestling)
if a wrestler accumulates a lead of 10 points or more, it is called a technical fall and that wrestler wins the match. Also known as technical superiority.

■ technical fouls or Ts (basketball)
procedural violations and misconduct that officials believe are detrimental to the game; penalised by a single free-throw opportunity to the non-offending team (2 free-throws and possession in college).

■ technical officials (weightlifting)

the competition officials, including the referees, jury, technical controllers, doping control officers and others.

■ technical points (wrestling)

points awarded during a match that help determine the outcome. The following system is used: Five points for a grand amplitude throw to an immediate position of danger; three points for taking the opponent from a standing position to an immediate position of danger; two points for a near fall; one point for a takedown, an escape, a reversal or for applying a correct hold without causing the opponent to touch the mat with head or shoulder. Not to be confused with classification points. See also *penalty points.*

■ technical superiority (wrestling)

a win by technical superiority is the same as a technical fall.

■ tekiyo (martial arts)

methods of self defense, including a variety of grabs, chokes and throws.

■ ten metre line (rugby)

one of the solid lines running across the field, 10 metres from the try-line.

■ tennis ball (lawn tennis)

the ball used in tennis is a hollow rubber sphere, 2 ½ to 2 5/8 inches in diameter and weighing between 2 and

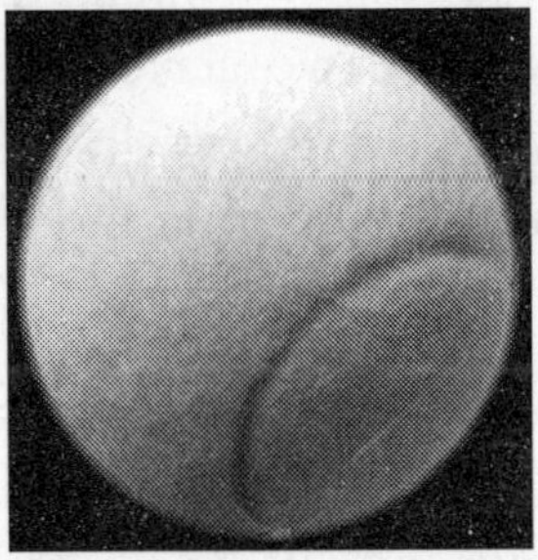

2 1/16 ounces, filled with pressurised air and covered with a nap of wool and nylon.

■ tennis elbow (lawn tennis)

tendinitis of the elbow, often caused by the strains placed on the joint by playing tennis, though it may have other causes.

■ **tens (rugby)**
a version of rugby with only ten players on a side. A half is usually ten minutes long.

■ **territory (football)**
the half of the field a team protects against its opponents.

■ **test (rugby)**
a match between two national teams.

■ **test match (cricket)**
an official two-inning match between two accredited national teams, usually spread over 5 playing days (30 hours).

■ **third-and-long (football)**
when the offense faces a third down and is more than a short running play away from a first down; usually third-and-5 or greater.

■ **third-ball attack (table tennis)**
a strategy in which the server attempts to win the point on the third ball over the net, almost invariably with a kill shot on the receiver's return of service.

■ **third-man-in rule (icehockey)**
the third man in a fight gets a game misconduct penalty and is out of the game for its duration; created to discourage players from jumping into a fight, even if they are only trying to break it up.

■ **third-party obstruction (field hockey)**
positioning oneself between the ball and an opponent, thereby allowing a teammate unobstructed access to the ball.

■ **thirty (lawn tennis)**
the second point scored by a player or side in a game. See *point; scoring system.*

■ **three prong (fencing)**
a type of epee body wire/connector; also an old-fashioned tip that would snag clothing, to make it easier to detect hits in the pre-electric era.

■ **three-day event (equestrian)**
a major series of tests in dressage, cross-country and jumping, conducted over a three-day period.

■ **three-on-one (icehockey)**
a type of break with three attackers coming in on one defenseman; this is a desperate situation.

■ **three-on-two (icehockey)**
a type of break with three attacking players skating against two defensive players.

■ **three-point position (equestrian)**
the basic riding position, so called because there are three points of contact with the saddle, both legs and the seat.

■ **throat (lawn tennis)**
the thin area of a racket handle, where it meets the head.

■ **throw (badminton)**
see *Carry*.

■ **throw (martial arts)**
any method of lifting the opponent from his feet and getting him to the ground.

■ **throw (wrestling)**
any move in which a wrestler lifts the opponent from the mat, then brings him back down.

■ **throw-in (basketball)**
the method by which a team with possession inbounds the ball.

■ **thrown point (fencing)**
a flick.

■ **thrust (fencing)**
an attack made by moving the sword parallel to its length and landing with the point.

■ **thumbless grip (weightlifting)**
a grip in which all four fingers and the thumb of the hand are on one side of the bar.

■ **tie-break (lawn tennis)**
a tiebreaker.

■ tiebreaker (lawn tennis)
a method of determining the winner of a set that's tied. The most commonly used is the 13-point tiebreaker, which is won by the player who first wins 7 points, provided that the margin of victory is at least 2 points. This is sometimes called a lingering death tiebreaker, on contrast to the sudden death tiebreaker.

■ tierce (fencing)
blade up and to the outside, wrist pronated.

■ tie-up (wrestling)
any move in which a wrestler grabs the opponent's upper body to gain control.

■ tight five (rugby)
the front and second rows, considered as a unit.

■ tighthead (rugby)
the No. 3 prop in a scrum. See also loosehead.

■ tilt (wrestling)
to turn the opponent so that his back goes from an angle of 45 degrees or more to less than 45 degrees.

■ time fault (equestrian)
a penalty for exceeding the time limit; ¼ fault is allotted for each second. In a jump-off, the penalty is one fault per second.

■ time hit (fencing)
also time-thrust; old name for stop hit with opposition.

■ time keeper (weightlifting)
an official who operates the timing clock; usually one of the three referees.

■ time trial (cycling)
a race in which riders or teams go around the track or course individually and the fastest time wins.

■ timeout (basketball)
when play is temporarily suspended by an official or at

the request of a team to respond to an injured player or discuss strategy; there are full timeouts (100 or 60 seconds in NBA, 120 seconds in WNBA, 75 or 60 seconds in college) and 20-second timeouts (30 seconds in college).

■ **time-wasting (field hockey)**
any action or non-action that keeps play from continuing or resuming within a reasonable period of time.

■ **timing clock (weightlifting)**
an electronic clock displayed on the attempt board that counts down the time that the current competitor has to make the lift. Allotted time ranges from one to two minutes; it's usually one and a half minutes in international competition.

■ **tip-off (basketball)**
the initial jump ball that starts the game.

■ **toe (rowing)**
to operate a rudder that's controlled by the foot.

■ **toe clips (cycling)**
clips or straps that securely fasten the rider's feet to the bicycle's pedals.

■ **ton or century (cricket)**
an individual score of 100 runs or more by a batter.

■ **tonfa (martial arts)**
originally the handle of a grinding wheel that used as a weapon by Okinawan peasants. The tonfa is most often used as a whirling instrument, swung by its handle, but the handle itself can also be used for attack.

■ **top position (wrestling)**
in par terre, the wrestler who is kneeling with hands on the

opponent's back is in the top position.

■ top seed (lawn tennis)
the player judged to be the best in a given tournament, usually on the basis of computer rankings. See *seed.*

■ topspin (lawn tennis)
forward spin, around the ball's horizontal axis that's applied by drawing the racket strings up and over the ball at the moment of impact. A shot hit with topspin is more likely to stay in play, because it drops sharply after reaching its highest point and it takes a high bounce.

■ topspin (table tennis)
forward spin applied by drawing the face of the paddle up across the ball at impact.

■ tori (martial arts)
generic term for the person performing a technique.

■ total (weightlifting)
the aggregate of the best good lifts in the snatch and the clean and jerk, which determines the competitor's ranking in the competition. If two competitors have the same total, the one with the lighter body weight is given the higher ranking.

■ touch (lawn tennis)
precise control of a shot, often resulting in a placement.

■ touch (rugby)
the ball is said to be in touch when it contacts or crosses a touch line or when the player carrying the ball steps out of bounds.

■ touch judge (rugby)
an official located on the side of the pitch to mark the spot where balls go out of touch and to judge kicks at goal. The touch judge may also call the referee's attention to violent infractions.

■ touchback (football)
when a player who gains possession of a ball in his own end zone kneels to the ground and automatically starts the next play at his own 20-yard line; also awarded if

his opponent kicks the ball across the end line.

■ **touchdown (TD) (football)**

when a team crosses the opponent's goal line with the ball, catches a pass in the opponent's end zone or recovers a loose ball in the opponent's end zone; earns a team 6 points.

■ **touch-line (rugby)**

a line that runs the length of the pitch and marks the side boundary.

■ **tournament (wrestling)**

A series of bouts to determine championships in various weight classes. A wrestler is eliminated after two losses. Elimination rounds continue until only three wrestlers remain in each pool. Finalists are seeded by classification points. If any of the finalists have not wrestled each other, they meet in a bout. Technical points or penalty points from previous matches are then carried over and added to the points accumulated in the final round.

■ **track (rowing)**

A U-shaped piece of metal that keeps the wheels of a seat on a straight path. A slide is made up of two tracks.

■ **track bike (cycling)**

a very simple bike used for track racing. It has a single-speed gear without free-wheeling and there are no brakes.

■ **track stand (cycling)**

The act of balancing the bicycle in place, with the feet on the pedals. In the match sprint, riders usually begin with a track stand, because each of them wants the other to set the pace in order to take advantage of the slipstream.

■ **trailer (icehockey)**

a player who follows his teammate on the attack seemingly out of the action but actually in a position to receive a backward or drop pass.

■ **transition (basketball)**
the shift from offense to defense.

■ **transition (equestrian)**
a change of pace or movement.

■ **trapping (field hockey)**
the act of stepping on the ball or covering it with the body; a violation.

■ **travelling (basketball)**
a floor violation when the ball handler takes too many steps without dribbling; also called walking.

■ **triple (baseball)**
a hit enabling the batter to safely reach third base.

■ **triple (lawn tennis)**
the feat of winning the singles, doubles and mixed doubles championships at a tournament.

■ **triple bar (equestrian)**
a jump that has three sets of rails at different heights.

■ **triple century (cricket)**
an individual score of 300 runs or more by a batter.

■ **triple double (basketball)**
when a player scores double-digits in 3 categories during one game (points, assists and rebounds are most common, but it can also be blocks or steals); a sign of great versatility.

■ **triple play (baseball)**
a defensive play that records 3 outs.

■ **tripping (icehockey)**
a minor penalty which occurs when a player places his stick or a part of his body under or around the feet or legs of an opponent causing him to lose his balance; will also be called if a player kicks an opponent's skates out from under him or uses

a knee or leg to cause his opponent to fall.

■ **trompement (fencing)**
deception of the parry.

■ **trot (equestrian)**
an easy gait in which the horse's legs move alternately in diagonal pairs; i.e., the right front and left rear legs, followed by the left front and right rear legs.

■ **try (rugby)**
a score, worth 5 points that's awarded when the ball is touched down by a player on the attacking side after it has been carried or kicked across the try-line. The scoring team is also awarded a conversion kick.

■ **try-line (rugby)**
a goal line, which extends across the pitch. The try-lines are a maximum of 100 metres apart.

■ **tsuki waza (martial arts)**
punching techniques.

■ **tuck (gymnastics)**
a position in which the body is folded at the waist, with the knees and hips bent and drawn into the chest.

■ **tunnel (rugby)**
the gap between the opposing front rows in a scrum or between the two lines of forwards in a lineout.

■ **turnover (basketball)**
when the offense loses possession through its own fault by passing the ball out of bounds or committing a floor violation.

■ **turnover (football)**
the involuntary loss of possession of the ball during a play, either by a fumble or by throwing an interception.

■ **twenty-two metre dropout (rugby)**
a kick from the 22-metre line, used to restart play after a missed penalty kick or drop goal has passed the dead-ball line or been touched down by a defending player. The ball is kicked back to the original attacking side.

■ twenty-two metre line (rugby)
one of the solid lines running across the field, 22 metres from the try-line.

■ twist (lawn tennis)
a combination of topspin and sidespin on a serve. See, for example, American twist and reverse twist.

■ twist (gymnastics)
a rotation of the body around the spine as the longitudinal axis.

■ two base hit (baseball)
a hit enabling the batter to safely reach second base. Also called a double.

■ two prong (fencing)
a type of body-wire/connector, used in foil and sabre.

■ two-colour rule (table tennis)
the rule that one of the paddle's striking surfaces must be black, the other red.

■ two-handed backhand (lawn tennis)
a backhand shot on which the player has both hands on the racket handle.

■ two-line pass (icehockey)
a type of offside violation occuring when a player passes the puck from his defending zone to a teammate across the red centre line, play is stopped for a face-off; also known as an offside pass.

■ two-metre line (water polo)
an imaginary line extending across the pool, two meters from each goal line.

■ two-metre man (water polo)
see *centre forward.*

■ two-meter violation (water polo)
an ordinary foul called when a player is inside the opponent's

two-metre line and is not behind the line of the ball.

■ **two-on-one (icehockey)**
a type of break with two attacking players skating against one defensive player.

■ **two-on-two (icehockey)**
a type of break with two attacking players skating against two defensive players.

■ **two-point position (equestrian)**
the position of the rider for a jump, with the seat out of the saddle and the body positioned forward.

■ **uchi waza (martial arts)**
striking techniques.

■ **ude garami (martial arts)**
an elbow hold that immobilises the opponent's arm. Literally, arm wrap.

■ **uke (martial arts)**
the person to whom a technique is applied; often taken to mean the opponent.

■ **uke waza (martial arts)**
techniques of blocking blows.

■ **ukemi waza (martial arts)**
techniques of rolling and falling safely.

■ **umpire (lawn tennis)**
the official who is in overall charge of a match. The umpire sits in a raised chair at one end of the net, calls the score after each point and has final responsibility for all questions of judgment and fact. He or she may reverse the decision of a judge or linesman if it is clearly in error and may impose point penalties or even default a player for unsportsmanlike conduct.

■ **under-led pass (icehockey)**
a pass behind or to one side of a teammate, making it difficult for him to control the puck.

■ underspin (lawn tennis)
see *backspin.*

■ uneven bars (gymnastics)
1) A piece of apparatus consisting of two bars, 148 centimetres and 228 centimetres high and a maximum of 150 centimetres apart. 2) A women's event performed on the apparatus, featuring swings, releases and regrasps and moves from one bar to the other.

■ unforced error (lawn tennis)
loss of a point caused by a poorly hit shot that goes into the net or out of the court. Compare *forced error.*

■ union (rugby)
the most common form of rugby, with 15 players on a side.

■ up and back (lawn tennis)
a doubles formation in which one partner plays in the forecourt, the other in the backcourt. Compare *tandem.*

■ up and under (rugby)
a high, shallow kick that gives the kicking side a good chance to run under and recover it. Also known as a Garryowen, for the Irish club that invented it.

■ up-and-back (badminton)
a doubles formation in which one partner is basically responsible for shots near the net, while the other is responsible for shots nearer the baseline.

■ upset (basketball)
when a higher-seeded (better) team loses to a lower-seeded (inferior) one.

■ **vasss (lawn tennis)**

acronym for the Van Alen Streamlined Scoring System, developed by James Van Alen. The main intent is to avoid the very long matches that can arise under the traditional scoring system. The Van Alen numbers the points from zero through four and awards a game to the first player to score four points, even if the other player has three points, thus eliminating deuce. Most important, Van Alen introduced the tiebreaker, which is now commonly used.

■ **vault (gymnastics)**

an event performed over the vaulting horse by both men and women. The gymnast races down a runway, vaults from a springboard onto the horse, landing with the hands and then vaults off to a standing position. Each competitor performs two vaults and the scores are averaged.

■ **vaulting horse (gymnastics)**

a piece of apparatus, 35 centimetres wide by 160 centimetres long, used for the vault. The men's vaulting horse is 135 centimetres high, the women's 120 centimetres high.

■ **velodrome (cycling)**

a track built specifically for bicycle racing, made up of two long straights and two short, curved end sections that are sharply banked. Most velodromes are 1/3 of a kilometre around, though some are as short as 200 metres and others as long as 500 metres.

■ **vertical (equestrian)**
a high obstacle.

■ **violation (basketball)**
see *floor violation.*

■ **virtuosity (gymnastics)**
the amount of rhythm and harmony displayed during a movement.

■ **volley (lawn tennis)**
a shot on which the ball is hit before it bounces. As a verb, to hit such a shot.

■ **volley (table tennis)**
to hit the ball before it has bounced. Illegal in table tennis; the offender loses the point.

■ **waffle pad (icehockey)**
a large rectangular pad attached to the front of the goalie's stick hand.

■ **wales conference (icehockey)**
was one of the two confrences in the NHL consisting of the Patrick and Adams Divisions until the 1992-93 season; renamed the Eastern Conference in 1993.

■ **walk (equestrian)**
the horse's slowest gait, in which the legs move individually in a diagonal pattern.

■ **walk the course (equestrian)**
to measure a jumping course by pacing off strides between obstacles before a competition.

■ **walk (baseball)**
an award given to the batter after the pitcher delivers 4

balls. If a hitter receives 4 balls during an at bat, they automatically advance to first base. Any forced base runners also advance. Also called base on balls.

■ **walkover (lawn tennis)**
a victory that results from the opponent's default.

■ **wall (equestrian)**
a jump that simulates a solid stone or brick wall.

■ **warm-up area (weightlifting)**
an area adjoining the competition stage where athletes warm up before attempting their lifts.

■ **wash out (icehockey)**
a goal that is ruled invalid by the referee or the waving off of an infraction by the linesmen.

■ **wash out (rowing)**
to bring the blade out of the water before the drive has been completed, thus losing power.

■ **water jump (equestrian)**
an obstacle that requires a horse to jump over a wide expanse of water, usually preceded by a low hedge or fence.

■ **waza ari awasete ippon (martial arts)**
a win in which the combatant has scored two waza-aris. (Judo).

■ **waza-ari (martial arts)**
a half win. Two waza-ari are equivalent to an ippon. (Judo and karate).

■ **weak side (water polo)**
the side of the pool opposite the side on which the ball is located.

■ **weakside (basketball)**
the side of the court away from the ball.

■ weakside (rugby)
the short side of a field on a ruck or maul. Also called the blindside.

■ weenie gear (cycling)
same as *granny gear.*

■ weigh-in (weightlifting)
the process of determining body weight for each competitor, which begins two hours before competition.

■ western conference (icehockey)
the renamed Cambell Conference beginning with the 1993-94 season which contains the Central, Northwest and Pacific Divisions.

■ wet pass (water polo)
a pass thrown so that it lands in the water.

■ wet shot (water polo)
a shot attempted by a player who is controlling the ball in the water; usually a quick wrist shot.

■ whip (equestrian)
a long, thin device held by the rider and used to urge the horse on.

■ whip back (gymnastics)
a movement similar to the back handspring, except that the hands don't touch the floor.

■ whip-over (fencing)
in sabre, a touch that results from the foible of the blade whipping over the opponent's guard or blade when parried.

■ whites (fencing)
fencing clothing.

■ wicket keeper (cricket)
the position equivalent to baseball's catcher.

■ wicket maiden (cricket)
a maiden over where one or more outs such as bowled or caught out also occur.

■ wicket (s) (cricket)
the terms wicket and wickets, are used in different and

important ways. the wicket is the strip of field between the two sets of sticks marking the bases, as in sticky wicket. A wicket, used as singular or plural, is a count of the number of outs in an inning, so 85 for 6 wickets means 85 runs scored, for 6 outs. the wickets, always used in plural, are the set of three sticks or stumps marking the base, as in He stood in front of the wickets. It helps to know the context in which the word is being used!

■ **wide (lawn tennis)**
descriptive of a shot that lands beyond the sideline or beyond the service sideline in the case of a serve. See also long.

■ **wide ball (cricket)**
a pitch that travels too far from the batter for him to have a reasonable chance of hitting it. The pitcher has to throw the pitch again and a penalty run is scored for the batting team.

■ **wild card (football)**
a team that makes the NFL playoffs by having one of the 2 best records among non-division winners in its conference.

■ **wild pitch (baseball)**
a pitch so far from the strike zone that the catcher cannot catch or block it, permitting any base runner to advance a base.

■ **win by x runs (cricket)**
the number of runs by which the team batting second falls short of the mark set by the first team, either because it has had 10 batters out or because (in a limited overs game) time ran out.

■ **win by x wickets (cricket)**
the number of wickets or outs that the team batting second has in hand when it passed the first team's total score. A win by 10 wickets, meaning no member of the second batting team was out, is an overwhelming victory: a win by one wicket, mean-

ing only the last out was left to the second team, a very narrow one !

■ **wind-out (cycling)**
a sprint that develops slowly, with gradual acceleration to top speed.

■ **wing (equestrian)**
a structure that frames a jump and supports the cups that hold the rails. A jump has two wings, one on each side.

■ **wing (field hockey)**
a forward who plays near the sideline. See also *inner*.

■ **wing (rugby)**
see *winger*.

■ **wing (water polo)**
an area near the sideline.

■ **wing forward (rugby)**
see *flanker*.

■ **winger (rugby)**
one of two backs, who usually wear Nos. 11 and 14. They're usually the fastest players on a side.

■ **wings (icehockey)**
two players who flank the centre on his right and left sides and, with him, make up the attacking unit or forward line.

■ **winner (lawn tennis)**
a shot that wins a point.

■ **Winning percentage (football)**
the percentage of its games a team has won during a period of time.

■ **women's doubles (table tennis)**
doubles competition between female teams.

■ **wood shot (badminton)**
a shot on which the frame of the racket strikes the base of the shuttle. Formerly illegal, but legalised in 1963.

■ **wood shot (lawn tennis)**
a shot on which the frame of the racket strikes the ball.

■ **wrist shot (icehockey)**
a shot made using a strong flicking of the wrist and forearm muscles, with the stick blade kept on the ice; it is

slower but more accurate than a slap shot.

■ **wrong-foot (lawn tennis)**
to hit a shot to the side of an opponent who is moving or turned in the other direction.

■ **yame (martial arts)**
stop; a command.

■ **yellow card (fencing)**
warning; used to indicate a minor rule infraction by one of the fencers.

■ **yellow card (field hockey)**
an intentional foul, such as rough play or a high stick, is penalised by suspending the player from the game for five minutes or longer. The penalty is signaled with a yellow card presented by the referee. The team plays short-handed, as in ice hockey, for the suspension period.

■ **yellow card (table tennis)**
a card that signifies a warning for a violation when shown to a player by the umpire. If shown along with a red card, it indicates that a penalty point has been awarded.

■ **yodan (martial arts)**
fourth-degree black belt.

■ **yoi (martial arts)**
ready.

■ **yorker (cricket)**
an overpitch delivery which is thrown so far forward as to bounce right under the batter's bat and beat him.

■ **yudansha (martial arts)**
one who holds a first degree black belt or higher.

■ **yuko (martial arts)**
a near waza-ari. However, yukos cannot be accumulated to make a higher score. (Judo).

■ **yurchenko (gymnastics)**
a mount for the vault, consisting of a roundoff onto the springboard, then a flic-flac onto the vault, followed by a back flip dismount. Named for Soviet gymnast Natalia Yurchenko, who created it.

■ yusei gachi (martial arts)

a win by superiority. (Judo).

■ zamboni (icehockey)

the brand of machine used to clean the ice.

■ zone (water polo)

a defense in which players are assigned to defend an area, rather than a specific opposing player.

■ zone defense (basketball)

a defense where each defender is responsible for an area of the court and must guard any player who enters that area; compare with man-to-man defense.

■ zones (icehockey)

three areas made up by the two blue lines; the attacking zone is the area farthest from the goal a player is defending; the neutral zone is the central area; the defending zone is the area where a player's goal is (the goal where his team's goalie is stationed).

Lotus Illustrated Dictionaries for Rs. 95 each

Agriculture

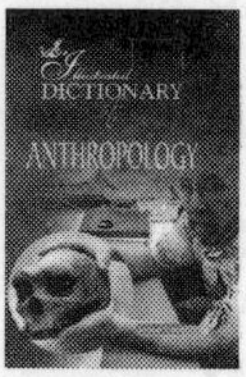

Anthropology

Architeture

Archaeology

Art

Astronomy

Banking Finance & Accounting

Business Administration

Bio Chemistry

Bio Technology

Biology

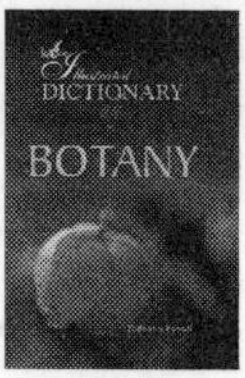

Botany

Chemical Engineering

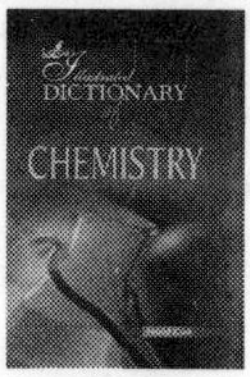

Chemistry

Civil Engineering

Computer Science

Commerce

Cooking & Food

Culture

Ecology

Other Books on

LOTUS ILLUSTRATED DICTIONARIES

1. Dictionary of New Words (New)	125/-
2. Dictionary of Veterinary Sciences (New)	125/-
3. Dictionary of Synonyms and Antonyms (New)	150/-
4. Dictionary of Idioms and Phrases (New)	150/-
5. First English Dictionary	125/-
6. Astronomy	125/-
7. Agriculture	125/-
8. Anthropology	125/-
9. Archaeology	125/-
10. Architecture	125/-
11. Art	125/-
12. Banking Finance & Accounting	125/-
13. Bio-Chemistry	125/-
14. Business Administration	125/-
15. Bio-Technology	125/-
16. Biology	125/-
17. Botany	125/-
18. Culture	125/-
19. Chemical Engg.	125/-
20. Chemistry	125/-
21. Civil Engineering	125/-
22. Computer Science	125/-
23. Commerce	125/-
24. Cooking & Food	125/-
25. Ecology	125/-
26. Economics	125/-
27. Education	125/-
28. Electrical Engineering	125/-
29. Electronic & Telecommunication	125/-
30. Environmental Studies	125/-
31. Festival	125/-
32. Geography	125/-

33. Geology	125/-
34. Genetic Engineering	125/-
35. Health & Nutrition	125/-
36. History	125/-
37. Import and Export	125/-
38. Information System Management	125/-
39. Internet	125/-
40. IT	125/-
41. Inorganic Chemistry	125/-
42. Law	125/-
43. Library & Information Science	125/-
44. Literature	125/-
45. Management	125/-
46. Mathematics	125/-
47. Marketing & Sales	125/-
48. Mass Communication	125/-
49. Mechanical Engg.	125/-
50. Medical	125/-
51. Music	125/-
52. Organic Chemistry	125/-
53. Philosophy	125/-
54. Physical Education	125/-
55. Physics	125/-
56. Psychology	125/-
57. Science	125/-
58. Sex	125/-
59. Sociology	125/-
60. Sports	125/-
61. Textile	125/-
62. Zoology	125/-

Lotus PRESS

Unit No. 220, Second Floor, 4735/22,
Prakash Deep Building, Ansari Road, Darya Ganj,
New Delhi - 110002, Ph.: 32903912, 23280047, 09811594448
E-mail: lotuspress1984@gmail.com, www.lotuspress.co.in

NOTES

Sports (206 pgs) F. No. 1